SMALL BUSINESS AND THE PUBLIC LIBRARY

D1283705

SMALL BUSINESS AND THE PUBLIC LIBRARY

Strategies for a Successful Partnership

LUISE WEISS
SOPHIA SERLIS-McPHILLIPS
ELIZABETH MALAFI

AMERICAN LIBRARY ASSOCIATION
CHICAGO   2011

Luise Weiss is the former head of adult reference and the Miller Business Resource Center at Middle Country Public Library in Centereach, New York. A graduate of Cornell University, she holds an MLS from the Palmer School of Library and Information Science and a BS from SUNY Stony Brook. Although retired, she works part-time at the Miller Business reference desk and teaches as an adjunct faculty member at the Palmer School. She has served as chair of ALA's BRASS Business References Sources committee and has been a member of the BRASS Business in Public Libraries committee.

Sophia Serlis-McPhillips is the coordinator of adult reference and the Miller Business Resource Center at the Middle Country Public Library. She earned a master's degree and a certificate in public library administration from the Palmer School, where she is an adjunct professor. She is on the NOVEL (New York Online Virtual Electronic Library) steering committee and has served on the ALA's BRASS Business in Public Libraries committee.

Elizabeth Malafi is the coordinator of adult programming and the Miller Business Resource Center at the Middle Country Public Library. She graduated with a BA from Hofstra University and earned her master's degree from the Palmer School, where she has since taught library science courses. She also serves on ALA's BRASS Business Reference Sources committee and contributes to the "Outstanding Business Reference Sources" column of *Reference and User Services Quarterly*. In 2008 she won the BRASS Dun & Bradstreet Public Librarian Support Award.

© 2011 by the American Library Association. Any claim of copyright is subject to applicable limitations and exceptions, such as rights of fair use and library copying pursuant to Sections 107 and 108 of the U.S. Copyright Act. No copyright is claimed for content in the public domain, such as works of the U.S. government.

Printed in the United States of America
15 14 13 12 11   5 4 3 2 1

Extensive effort has gone into ensuring the reliability of the information in this book; however, the publisher makes no warranty, express or implied, with respect to the material contained herein.

ISBN: 978–0-8389–0993–5 (paper); 978-0-8389-9322-4 (PDF); 978-0-8389-9323-1 (ePub); 978-0-8389-9324-8 (Mobipocket); 978-0-8389-9325-5 (Kindle). For more information on digital formats, visit the ALA Store at alastore.ala.org and select eEditions.

Library of Congress Cataloging-in-Publication Data
Weiss, Luise, 1937-
 Small business and the public library : strategies for a successful partnership / Luise Weiss, Sophia Serlis-McPhillips, and Elizabeth Malafi.
    p.   cm.
 Includes bibliographical references and index.
 ISBN 978-0-8389-0993-5 (alk. paper)
 1. Libraries and business—United States. 2. Libraries and the unemployed—United States. 3. Business information services—United States. I. Serlis-McPhillips, Sophia. II. Malafi, Elizabeth. III. Title.
 Z711.75.W45 2011
 021.2—dc23
                                                                           2011022354

Book design in Aller, Union, and Minion Pro by Casey Bayer.
Cover images © track5/TommL/endopackendopack/ericsphotography/monkeybusinessimages/iStockphoto®

♾ This paper meets the requirements of ANSI/NISO Z39.48–1992 (Permanence of Paper).

CONTENTS

1/12

PREFACE

An ALA news release of October 29, 2008, entitled "ALA Seeks $100 Million in Stimulus Funding as U.S. Libraries Face Critical Cutbacks, Closures" cited the need for libraries to "expand critical employment activities and services such as resume development, job bank web searches, and career planning workshops." On December 12, a segment of the *NBC Nightly News* with Brian Williams stressed the benefits that libraries offer in these challenging economic times.

In addition, much of the current library literature cites the need for libraries to remain relevant and to adapt to changing times. When this book was started—a few years ago—the economy appeared to be flourishing. Today—as we begin the twenty-first century's second decade—we are facing a historic economic crisis. Reports about increasing job losses and massive unemployment are daily news. One way libraries can stay relevant in these conditions is by addressing the needs of job seekers, working families, new immigrants, college applicants, and the small business community. In the past few months, the Miller Business Resource Center (MBRC) has seen an increasing number of patrons requesting assistance with resume preparation. Many are experiencing unemployment for the first time in their adult lives. Others are reentering the workforce to supplement the family income. Prospective college students are dealing with financial aid problems as their parents' college funds have evaporated. Businesses are facing hard times and are seeking new marketing and networking solutions.

A number of public libraries have incorporated small business services within their libraries. Over the years, the Middle Country Public Library (MCPL) in Centereach, New York, and the Miller Business Resource Center within it have established a series of local and regional partnerships, networking alliances, collections, services, and personnel to assist patrons with many business and employment issues. Some of the programs offered have been in place for years. Others have evolved recently in cooperation with local and regional partnerships. What we find is successful, we try to duplicate and improve. A sampling of programs includes:

SAT and PSAT preparation classes. The cost of many SAT and PSAT preparation classes can be prohibitive for families trying to save for college tuition. For over twenty-five years, the MCPL has offered two workshops; a PSAT preparation workshop in the fall and an SAT workshop in the winter. These consist of five 2½-hour sessions, and the cost is fifteen dollars for the PSAT or SAT preparation guide. Sixty students can take each course. The teachers are hired by the library, and the funds come from the programming budget.

Career counseling, resume and interview preparation. Career counselors are available three nights per week, two weekdays, and Saturdays to help district residents with job resumes, interview preparation, interest inventories, and college guidance. The counselors, all of whom have advanced degrees, are hired on a part-time basis. Counseling sessions are on a one-to-one basis and take approximately forty-five minutes.

Job fairs. The Miller Center hosts two job fairs each year in conjunction with the Suffolk County Department of Labor; each fair attracts 30 employers and over 300 job seekers. These events are sponsored and funded by the Department of Labor and give local area residents a chance to come to their home library and investigate possible job opportunities.

ESOL and citizenship classes. The Miller Center offers a number of programs to help new immigrants to enhance their workforce preparation skills. ESOL classes are offered to help non-English speakers learn listening, speaking, reading, and writing

English skills. Citizenship classes help to explain the various naturalization processes and to prepare for the U.S. citizenship test. Often, the professional licenses of new residents are not valid in the United States and recertification is required. Citizenship classes and career counseling classes assist people in negotiating this recertification process. An additional program, Conversation Groups, facilitates networking among people new to the United States.

Library Business Connection. For over eight years, Library Business Connection meetings have served as a networking forum for the local business community. Speakers on a variety of business topics from e-commerce to time management have imparted business wisdom and know-how. Membership continues to grow because local networking provides marketing leads and business support. In this unpredictable economic climate, these free and informative networking meetings at the library may be the best business value in town.

In writing *Small Business and the Public Library,* we have tried to highlight various series of steps and action plans in creating a business resource center within a public library. The chapters in this book will detail ideas on collection development, programming, marketing techniques, and coalition and partnership building that can be adopted and adapted to grow a small business and finance collection into a vital regional business resource that is part of a public library.

From the sidewalk lemonade stand to the giant corporation, every business wants to find more customers. *Who are they? How do I identify them? How do I reach them?* The job seeker also has questions. *Where can I find a job? What skills will I need?* Increasingly, public libraries have gained access to current demographic and marketing data that are of real value to the business and job-hunting community. How do we create public awareness of these resources and services? In *Small Business and the Public Library: Strategies for a Successful Partnership,* we seek to identify the key elements of a public library's business and career services and suggest ways of marketing them to the business community through innovative programming, active networking, and mutually beneficial partnerships.

Chapter 1 explores how a robust library business service brings benefits to both the business community and the library, and discusses both the role of technology in facilitating the service and the vital importance of outreach in achieving a working relationship between the library and local businesses. Chapter 2 identifies those resources, both print and electronic, that have proved the most valuable in answering business and career questions. Chapter 3 discusses the unique issues involved in creating programs for a business audience. Chapter 4 stresses the importance of marketing to a successful library business service. Networking and its critical role in establishing business connections is the subject of chapter 5. Chapter 6 studies how partnerships can contribute to innovative marketing and programming, and chapter 7 investigates ways of acquiring funding.

Acknowledgments

We are grateful to those librarians across the country who graciously gave their time and expertise to answer our questions, including:

Misty Jones and Amanda Hollings, Charleston County Library, Charleston, SC

Tonya Badillo, Long Branch Free Public Library, Long Branch, NJ

Nancy Johnson and Ellen Meyers, Newton Public Library, Newton, MA

Joan Divor, Burlington County Public Library, Westampton, NJ

Laura Bernheim, Waltham Public Library, Waltham, MA

Deb Weltsch, Poughkeepsie Public Library, Poughkeepsie, NY

Kara Stock, Buffalo and Erie County Public Library, Buffalo, NY

Elaine Sozzi, Westchester Library System, Westchester County, NY

Michael Buhmann, Skokie Public Library, Skokie, IL

Bonnie Easton, Cuyahoga County Public Library, Parma, OH

Pamela Jenkins, Kansas City Public Library, Kansas City, MO

Bernice Kao, Fresno County Public Library, Fresno, CA

Jennifer Keohane, Simsbury Public Library, Simsbury, CT

Laura Metzger and Carol Starzmann, Cecil County Public Library, Elkton, MD

Sal DiVincenzo, Middle Country Public Library, Centereach, NY

To J. Michael Jeffers, publisher extraordinaire at ALA Editions, we extend our heartfelt gratitude for his unbelievable patience and kindness with our interminable delays and wish him a future of authors who keep deadlines.

Writing this book has allowed us to reflect not only on our careers as business librarians but also on the role that business librarians have played in the public library. When we entered the field of library and information science, we never imagined that this would be the path that we would follow and how fortunate we were to become involved with the development of the Miller Business Resource Center. We would like to thank the following people without whom this book could not have been written: Sandra Feinberg, director of the Middle Country Public Library, an innovative and progressive leader who has challenged us to attain our goals and who gave us the freedom to explore new ideas and programs; Barbara Jordan, assistant director for community relations at the Middle Country Public Library (now retired), for her tireless efforts, grant writing, and for embracing the concept of the Miller Business Resource Center; the Middle Country Library Foundation, for fostering the growth of the Miller Business Resource Center; the Miller Business Resource Center team for their professionalism, devotion, and enthusiasm; the MCPL Community Relations Department for their constant support and assistance with all of our programs and events; John D. Miller for his continuous support and for recognizing the need to develop a regional business center on Long Island; and all of our community partners for their trust and for sharing a common passion.

We would also like to thank all of our colleagues for sharing their knowledge, experiences, and thoughts as well as taking time out from their busy schedules to respond to all our inquiries.

Business Services and the Mission of the Library

T imes Are Tough, Libraries Are Thriving" announced a *New York Times* headline of March 15, 2009. Today, as we mark the beginning of the twenty-first century's second decade, we are facing a historic economic crisis. Massive job losses and stubbornly high unemployment are daily news. Meanwhile, much of the current library literature cites the need for libraries to remain viable and adapt to changing times. How can we do this? Is it possible? One way libraries are staying relevant is by addressing the needs of job seekers, working families, new immigrants, college applicants, and the small business community. It is, after all, the small business sector of the U.S. economy that has generated 60–80 percent of new jobs annually over the last decade, and small businesses employ 50 percent of the private sector workforce.

As businesses face hard times and loss of revenue, they constantly seek new avenues to increase their sales, marketing efforts, and networking opportunities. The time is right for the public library to recognize that the business community should be an integral part of the library's marketing focus. Advances in technology have made it possible for public libraries to assist businesses in ways never before possible. Business databases accessible to libraries allow entrepreneurs to

> pinpoint existing customers
> target new customers
> identify and evaluate competition
> locate industry benchmarks and forecasts
> examine retail sales and consumer expenditure data for any U.S.
> > zip code

evaluate the local, regional, and national business climate
study market trends through marketing research reports

The following example demonstrates how libraries often have access to data that today's search engines cannot find and how more and more business information is becoming available all the time. One aspect remains constant, however—the need for a trained librarian who knows who produces the information and where to find it.

When electronic resources and the Internet first became widely available, an exasperated MBA student approached the librarian at the reference desk of the Middle Country Public Library. He explained that he had spent nearly two fruitless hours searching the Web for a desperately needed pie chart of sneaker sales and he had found nothing. Within a few minutes, the librarian presented the relieved student with a Standard & Poor's Industry Survey entitled "Apparel and Footwear: Retailers and Brands" with the elusive pie chart (then, still in paper format) and also the URL of the website of the National Sporting Goods Association.

Today, we can offer even more. Standard & Poor's industry surveys are now online, and we also have the Sports Business Research Network database, which can give 15 years of sales data for over 20 different types of athletic footwear with consumer expenditures by brand, age group, education level of household head, gender, geographic region, household income, outlet type, and price point, as well as future trends and forecasts.

Most of the time businesses are unaware of the existence of these resources or that the public library of today might have them available. Traditionally, the local merchant does not associate the public library with business assistance. Entrepreneurs envisioning a business library usually picture one connected to a business school, a major city, or a corporate headquarters. The public library is equated with "homework help" and recreational reading. In the past three decades, however, the explosion of data being gathered and stored electronically has paved the way for access to a wealth of specialized business information. In the late 1980s, public libraries' holdings usually did not contain more than twenty business magazines and journals, in paper, with some microfilmed back issues. Today, one business periodical database alone affords full-text access to over 2,300 business magazines and journals whose contents can be e-mailed, faxed, and even remotely retrieved. Twenty years ago, the average library had a few directories of major U.S. businesses. Currently directory databases of over 15 million U.S. businesses provide entries by company name, sales volume, staff size, zip code, and Standard Industrial Classification (SIC) and North American Industry Classification System (NAICS) code.

Businesses also need market research data to help them determine product development, future marketing strategies, and accurate pricing. In the past, market research data have often proved either elusive to obtain or too costly for the small entrepreneur. Market research generally is divided into two categories: primary and secondary research. Primary research is most often gathered through interviews, focus groups, direct mail, telemarketing, and so on and is usually collected to address a specific problem or issue. Done either in-house or by a paid market researcher, these reports often carry a price tag of thousands of dollars. Secondary research is data that is already compiled and/or published information. It often tracks trends within a market, industry, or geographic or demographic segment. It can include market research reports, company profiles, articles from trade journals, and publications from government agencies, trade organizations and associations, and commercial publishers.

Technological advances have greatly multiplied the number and quality of business data resources the average public library can now offer the business sector. Technology has also made possible the increased speed with which data can be gathered and made accessible. Large vendors to "big box" stores such as Home Depot and Wal-Mart can receive daily—sometimes even hourly—reports on how their products are selling. While that data are not usually available to the small vendor, there are many secondary data market reports that are synthesized synopses of the raw data. Access to online proprietary databases, government statistical data, industry market research, and association reports has allowed libraries to tap into previously cost-prohibitive and unavailable resources and make them available to the business community. Librarians are experts at searching for and locating information, and businesses can profit greatly from this expertise.

The competitive edge needed to achieve continuous growth in today's knowledge-based economy requires access to timely, accurate, and relevant information and the acquisition of skills and competencies to effectively use that information. The business owner, equipped with this information, has an edge in the challenging marketplace. Conversely, small businesspeople who lack both an awareness and access to these unique industry resources find themselves at a distinct disadvantage in the information-driven business arena.

Small Business and the Public Library seeks to discuss *library recognition of the business community as potential library users and the elimination of barriers to service.* It is, quite simply, in the library's best interest to cultivate the business community as library users. Their success is crucial to the continued economic health of the neighborhood the library serves. When the library recognizes the businessperson as library patron, the benefits can be mutual. The businessperson gains needed industry data and marketing assistance to strengthen his operation. The library gains a supportive, appreciative patron who can often be counted on to sponsor library events and help promote the library's business center. And, as we have found, in addition to contributing to community economic strength, the business community has come to recognize our library as a strong force in melding the local spheres of influence. The library can serve as neutral territory for the private, governmental, and public sectors to address common concerns.

Libraries must recognize that mandating a patron's actual presence in a library and restricting librarians to in-house presentations and service and even to rigid schedules create barriers to service. Business librarians must be encouraged to meet businesspeople "on their own turf" and to give presentations at Chambers of Commerce and local business groups to demonstrate available resources. Schedules need to be adjusted to facilitate professionals' attendance at "business before hours" or evening meetings, and librarians need to be prepared to present practical, concrete examples of what the business library can offer. To most people, the term *database* is intimidating and conjures up images of an endless learning curve. The librarian who demonstrates how the library's database can provide a list of every business in the community ranked by sales and number of employees will surely capture a business audience's interest. The combination of a business resource with high-priority information and the librarian's speed and skill in accessing it has offered the entrepreneur a marketing tool that could increase his bottom line. And, of equal importance, he has associated this information with a real person—a professional who has demonstrated an awareness of the needs of his business and a willingness to assist him in helping it to grow and prosper.

In succeeding chapters, we will explore ways to broaden our knowledge of business information needs and to increase the use of business resources through partnerships and networks and to expand the potential to provide a greater variety of resources through shared costs. We will explore how formal and informal networks and partnerships can further promote the library's credibility as a key regional resource for business information and a factor in economic success.

In career centers across the country, librarians are forming partnerships with business organizations, government agencies, and nonprofits to inform job seekers of their libraries' resources. Library websites are becoming clearinghouses of information as they provide links to job sites, civil service test announcements and applications, sample online career tests, career counseling, and unemployment assistance.

Moreover, responding to reference queries from multiple industry sectors rather than just a few cannot help but sharpen librarians' skills and increase their awareness of business information needs. And additional revenue received through partnerships and networks broadens the selection of resources and services a library can make available to its local business patrons.

The importance of networking can be seen in the following account of a recent reference encounter. The Small Business Development Center (SBDC), an arm of the Small Business Administration (SBA) based at the State University of New York at Stony Brook, sent Kim, a young woman starting a real estate photography business, to our business reference desk for help. Originally, Kim was only looking for a contract form she could modify for dealing with real estate agencies. She left with a few books on managing a commercial photography business and an e-mailed Excel spreadsheet of all the real estate agencies in surrounding zip codes, as well as her contract forms. Kim might never have found us without the intermediation and recommendation of the SBDC.

Small Business and the Public Library examines how public libraries are reaching out to the business community and marketing their services. We explore practical strategies and procedures that you can use to start or improve a business service within your library. It is important to realize that establishing a service to businesses takes time. For the three of us, Sophia, Elizabeth, and Luise, our principal library experience has been in the Middle

Country Public Library in Centereach, New York, where we have been involved in the twenty-year process of building the Miller Business Resource Center. What started as a small business and finance collection and a pilot career-counseling project has grown to a 5,000-square-foot resource center which includes reference and circulating business, finance, law, and career information collections, dedicated business computers, a reading area of new business best sellers and periodicals, a meeting room, and several small conference rooms and offices for the business and career information staff, as well as shared office space utilized by the local Chamber of Commerce, the Stony Brook Small Business Development Center, and others.

In 1999 the Middle Country Library Foundation and the Hauppauge Industrial Association (HIA), a 1,100-member regional industrial association, received a $50,000 legislative grant to develop a plan for the library's Business Resource Center to provide business research services and access to specialized business databases to HIA members. Over the past twelve years, the partnership has continued to grow. In addition to providing one-on-one research, Miller Business Resource Center business librarians routinely present workshops to the HIA membership, take part in HIA committees, help develop website content, and participate in the HIA Annual Trade Show.

In May 2000, when Miller Business Resource Center librarians set up their booth at the HIA Annual Trade Show, attendees asked repeatedly, "Why would a public library display at a trade show?" As we demonstrated the database access that HIA members received through the partnership, they were surprised and intrigued. Now, when we attend the trade show each May, we are hailed on a first-name basis. We invariably leave with a new round of business research questions but also with the knowledge that we are an integral part of the HIA organization.

Providing personalized business reference and research services for approximately fifty people per day via on-site visits, phone, fax, and e-mail requests for assistance, the Miller Business Resource Center addresses the business needs of about 12,000 patrons per year. Topics include market research, industry trends, supplier and distributor information, sales and import/export particulars, demographic and statistical data, and laws and regulations. A range of special databases for the regional business community and the center's many business partners are accessible via the center's website, www.millerbusinesscenter.org.

While researching material for this publication, we reexamined the development of the Miller Business Resource Center and explored business resources in very large public libraries such as the New York Public Library's Science, Industry and Business Library and the Brooklyn Public Library, as well as smaller urban and suburban area libraries such as the Charleston County Public Library in Charleston, South Carolina, and the Burlington County Library in Burlington, New Jersey. We have spoken to jobs and careers librarians in towns and cities from Massachusetts to California. We would like to share with the library and nonprofit community the many original programs and unique collections we have seen, as well as the creative marketing ideas, resourceful fund-raising strategies, and powerful networking and partnership coalitions that have captured the interest of the business and library community.

2

Collection Development
Tools of the Trade

What type of materials should you look for to build a public library business collection? Often, the best place to start is by reviewing the business questions you are asked. Were you able to answer all of them? Are there resources that would have helped?

Some of the typical questions that business librarians report receiving most often sound something like this:

> Where can I find a list of all the pharmaceutical companies in my area?
>
> I am a landscaper. I want to secure the grounds contract for the office building at 150 Main Street. Where can I find out who owns the building?
>
> For my business plan, I need to find the demographics for the zip codes I plan to service. Can you help me find them?
>
> I am interviewing for a job in the plastics industry. Can you give me an industry survey and some questions I might ask or be asked?
>
> What is the average hourly wage for carpenters in Kalamazoo, Michigan?

Do these sound familiar? How can a public library develop a business collection to answer these questions and many more? What are the priorities? Can we use some free materials?

An information request we have been hearing a lot lately starts like this:

> I have always wanted to be my own boss. Since the job market is so poor and I have recently become unemployed, I am seriously considering starting my own business. However, I don't know where to begin. Can you help me?

Quite often, the people asking are highly qualified individuals who are having difficulty finding reemployment at the same level as their previous position, or they want to open a part-time business to supplement their income. However, they lack expertise in starting and running a business.

Starting a landscaping business in Lancaster County, Pennsylvania, may be different from starting one in Corpus Christi, Texas. And the regulatory requirements for a new eco-friendly lawn service might not be the same in Lexington, Kentucky, as in Westport, Connecticut. Many prospective entrepreneurs are unaware of all the issues involved in opening a new business.

All states are anxious to encourage small business development within their jurisdictions. The U.S. Small Business Administration (www.sba.gov) offers links to business name registration, tax revenue agencies, and license and permit regulations for all U.S. states. Often, local town and county home pages also offer business development guides for their area.

If you are considering writing your own business development guide, you might consider meeting with town and county officials to assist in creating one. For help identifying the major issues involved in a small business start-up, an excellent example is *Keys to Starting a Business in Cecil County*, developed by the Small Business Information Center (SBIC) of the Cecil County Public Library (CCPL) in Elkton, Maryland (figure 2.1).

An e-mail from Carol Starzmann, CCPL assistant director, explained that a meeting of community leaders resulted in the SBIC librarian taking on the responsibility of creating the brochure, which has since become a library best seller. Its excellence was also recognized by the State Library Resource Center, and it was adapted for distribution and featured on the Pratt Library website. However, Starzmann advises that readers should understand that the brochure is to be used primarily as a teaching tool for beginner business guidance.

In keeping with the focus of a public library business collection to provide prospective entrepreneurs with the information resources to help start their new venture, once a month, in our library, a business librarian teaches the information-gathering segment of a Community Development Corporation (CDC) entrepreneurship class for prospective business owners. In order to receive financial assistance from the CDC, the class members must develop business plans for their proposed enterprises. The librarians showcase available resources to help them identify their plans, access demographics, locate

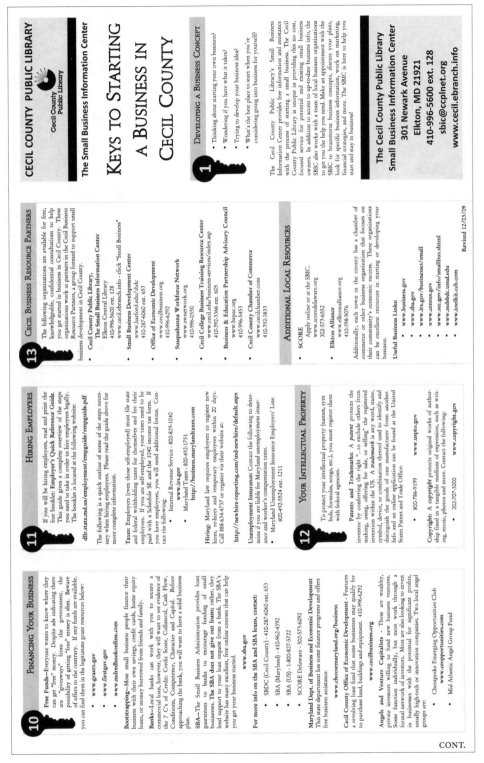

FIGURE 2.1 A business development guide can offer quick, location-specific information while introducing the community to your services.

2 Forming a Legal Business Structure

Before you register as a business, you must determine your legal ownership structure and file with the state. Differences, benefits and costs of each can be viewed at:

http://sba.gov/smallbusinessplanner/start/choosestructure/START_FORMS_OWNERSHIP.html

The legal structures are:

- **Sole Proprietorships or Partnerships**—no legal filing required for entity to exist, other than a business permit.
- **Limited Partnership, Limited Liability Company, Limited Liability Partnerships, or Corporation**—must file with the Maryland State Dept. of Assessment and Taxation.

Information on the advantages and disadvantages of each can be found in books at the library, and in an online state publication: *Guide to Legal Aspects of Doing Business in Maryland*, located at:

http://www.oag.state.md.us/legalaspects.pdf

3 Registering a Business Name

Your business needs to register with the State of Maryland. An online database lets you search to see if your name is available or actively being used. The business name database is under the Maryland Department of Assessments and Taxation at:

www.dat.state.md.us

Click on "Business Data Search," then "Business Data Search" again, then "Business Entity". Once you've determined an available business name and chosen a legal structure, you can register online at the above web address

4 Getting an EIN from the IRS

410-767-1340.

An EIN (Employer Identification Number), known as a Federal Tax ID Number, is obtained from the IRS. Look under "businesses" at www.irs.gov to determine if you will need an EIN.

If your business requires one, you can download the form at:

www.irs.gov/pub/irs-pdf/fss4.pdf

You must know what your legal business structure will be before you apply for an EIN. You can apply online, by phone, or through the mail:

FAX: 631-447-8960
TEL: 800-829-4933

5 Business Licenses and More

Business licenses, certifications and permits can be confusing because requirements vary from business to business. The best plan is to contact the following agencies and explain what kind of business you are planning. They will help you to determine what you need to do to be "legal".

- County Clerk of the Circuit Court—410-996-5375
- The Dept. of Permits and Inspections—410-996-5235
- The Cecil County Health Department—410-996-5550

Many businesses also need to register with the state of Maryland. You can do so by phone at 888-218-5925 or online:

http://www.dllr.state.md.us/license

6 Maryland Business Taxes

Information about business taxes in Maryland can found at the following website:

http://business.marylandtaxes.com

You must register with the state for paying your business taxes. If you use the Maryland Combined Registration Online Application at the website below, it will include your business accounts for income tax withholding, sales and use tax, and unemployment insurance. Go to:

interactive.marylandtaxes.com/webapps/comptrollercra/entrance.asp

Other tax and business application forms can be found at:

www.dat.state.md.us/sdatweb/sdatforms.html

The local tax office in Cecil County is at:
103 Chesapeake Blvd., Elkton, MD 21921; 410-996-0580.

7 Contacting Regulatory Agencies

Zoning and Building:
Make sure your business site is zoned for the kind of business activity you intend for the property.

Cecil County Dept. of Planning and Zoning
129 East Main Street, Room 300
Elkton, MD 21921
410-996-5220

Environmental:
Determine if there are any regulations (air pollution, water discharge, waste, etc.) protecting the environment that you need to correct on your property, or that you need to properly prepare for in your business production.

Maryland Dept. of the Environment
1800 Washington Blvd., Baltimore, MD 21230
800-633-6101
www.mde.state.md.us

Health:
Businesses involving, preparing food for sale or providing health services for people require special health regulations and inspections.

Cecil County Health Dept.
401 Bow Street, Elkton MD 21921
410-996-5550
www.cecilcountyhealth.org

Safety:

Maryland Occupational Safety & Health
1100 N. Eutaw Street
Baltimore, MD 21201
410-767-2189
www.dllr.state.md.us/labor/mosh.html

Federal OSHA
820 First Street, NE
Washington, DC 20020
202-693-5000
www.osha.gov

8 Writing Your Business Plan

A business plan is the foundation to making your business work. Lenders, potential investors, and other business professionals will want to see your business plan, especially if you are trying to get a loan. Even if you aren't seeking financing, a business plan is your blueprint for success. It's hard work to write a business plan, but well worth the effort as statistics show that a business plan can make a significant difference between a business thriving or dying.

A typical business plan is about 20 pages long and details the following topics: Executive Summary; Business Description; Management; Market Analysis and Strategy; Customers and Competitors; Operations; and Financial Analysis.

The library has many books, workshops, outlines, and individual consultations available to help you to prepare your business plan. An online guide can be found at:

www.score.org/template_gallery.html

Sample Business Plans—we also carry sample business plans in our reference collection in the Small Business Information Center office and online at our website:

http://www.cecil.ebranch.info/small-business/

9 Insurance for Your Business

- Consider getting coverage for property damage, liability and business interruptions
- Investigate specialty insurance for your particular business
- Contact the state insurance agency about any problems

Maryland Insurance Administration
525 St. Paul Place, Baltimore, MD, 21202
800-492-6116
www.mdinsurance.state.md.us

Feeling overwhelmed? Let us help you!

The Small Business Information Center at the Cecil County Public Library
301 Newark Ave., Elkton, MD 21921 • 410-996-5600 ext. 128
sbic@ccplnet.org • www.cecil.ebranch.info

FIGURE 2.1 (cont.)

relevant trade publications and associations, and identify key business ratios. They demonstrate the features of both print and online resources and encourage class members to use the library's databases and software business plan program. Teaching this course has given us insight into what resources are needed for a business collection.

Business Plans

As Robert Pankl asserts, "The public library is virtually the only place aspiring entrepreneurs can go for the information to fill in the blanks in the business plan. It has the appropriate reference resources to give meaning and utility to the *demographics* and *competitors,* and other terms used with a clear idea of what they mean and their relevance to specific situations. The appropriate reference sources identify who and where they are" (Pankl 2010, 96). Business plans call for identifying the demographics of a business's target market, including population, average age, income, and education. Also important are psychographics that measure attitudes, values, lifestyles, and opinions. The resources that cover these areas are treated as follows.

Demographic and Psychographic Data

Demographics Now—Geared for marketing and business plans, this Cengage Learning database provides demographic estimates, consumer expenditures, and retail sales potential for all levels of U.S. geography and allows users to generate maps and reports.

SRDS Local Market Audience Analyst—Providing market analysis for 210 DMAs (designated market areas) and more than 3,000 U.S. counties, this database generates market profile, lifestyle analyst, and demographic reports. It also gives insight into the lifestyle traits and behavior of target market groups.

U.S. Lifestyles is a *ReferenceUSA* database wherein users can search by geography, household income, home value, and nineteen different lifestyles (i.e. catalog shopper, health/fitness) for over 100 million individuals.

An annual Nielsen Claritas and D&B product, *MPA: Market Profile Analysis: Consumer and Business Demographic Reports,* reviews demographic and market data for specific U.S. geographic regions. Population, households, education, and labor force factors are given down to census-tract level, and industry, occupational, and business market factors are given down to zip-code level. Business market factors specify numbers of companies by employee range and sales/volume ranges for each zip code by 20 primary NAICS classifications.

American Factfinder—http://factfinder.census.gov—is a free site that includes detailed census information from the federal government. As the 2010 census data is entered, this site will become more current. It does, however, contain data tables from the American Community Survey that tracks changing communities on an annual basis. Population and housing information is updated yearly while age, race, income, commute time to work, home value, veteran status, and other variables are collected for different locations on three- and five-year cycles.

Sample Business Plans

Whether starting a new business, seeking funds for expansion, or mapping the future direction of an existing enterprise, a business plan can be a powerful means of communicating with investors, bankers, marketers, and staff. Sample business plans are often in high demand by those who are trying to create one. Sources for these include the following ones.

Business Plan Pro is a Palo Alto Software program, issued annually, that contains over 500 customizable sample business plans and 9,000 industry profiles. Included are business valuation analyses, cash flow planning, plan outlines for nonprofits, and SBA-approved document forms.

Business Plans Handbook—A Gale Cengage Learning print and online series with over 400 sample business plans created by real-life entrepreneurs. Recent plans include those for an art gallery, a microbrewery, an organic food store, a health care marketing agency, a home repair and improvement company, a pet-sitting service, and a plus-size children's clothing store.

Small Business Resource Center—A Gale Cengage Learning database, it covers all major areas of starting and operating a business, including accounting, financing, franchising, human resources, management, marketing, and taxes. Included are all volumes of the *Business Plans Handbook* as well as a number of titles from the "For Dummies" series.

Industry Surveys

First Research—A Hoover's/Dun & Bradstreet database, it profiles approximately 700 industries in 20- to 25-page reports covering industry overviews, recent developments, business challenges, executive insights, financials with company benchmark information, and an extensive list of industry-oriented call prep questions that are useful for salespeople and job seekers.

Standard & Poor's Net Advantage—Although primarily reporting on public companies, this S&P database contains 55 industry surveys focusing on profiles and trends, key ratios and statistics and comparative analyses, as well as segments on how the industry operates and analyses of a featured industry company.

Directories

Directories are essential tools, not only for the new business owner but also for marketers, salespeople, job seekers, fund-raisers, and others looking to pinpoint customers, competition, employers, and potential donors. Libraries serious about a business service should consider purchasing a subscription to at least one comprehensive business directory such as *Dun's Global Access* or *ReferenceUSA.* While a significant expense, these directories provide major marketing and employment leads.

Directories are also very useful for learning about the business concentrations in your area and for establishing your credentials with the business community. With access to one of the directory databases such as *D&B Total U.S. Million Dollar Database* or *ReferenceUSA,* you can generate a listing of all the businesses in your community with contact names. Try sorting the list by sales volume, number of employees, type of business, and so on. If you have GPS software such as Microsoft Map Point, you might also want to produce a community map with business locations. Area lists also give you a breakdown of the different industries in your area.

Armed with these lists, try visiting your local banks. Often, you will find that banks have one or two people in charge of business accounts. We have found that a list of local businesses is very well received by them. We are now asked regularly to produce these lists. Recently, the regional head of the business liaisons for one large bank came and requested lists for a new branch employee. We asked him about the bank's own directory product. He explained that our directory was far more robust than the bank's limited version. In addition, he continued, we saved him so much time and effort! Local bankers need to get out into the community, and it is definitely an asset to have them "in your camp."

Patrons are often amazed that these databases exist, and they are delighted when they hear that the information can be delivered to their desktops via an Excel spreadsheet with all the businesses in a given zip code or a certain SIC code or NAICS code, which includes pertinent directory-type information. Job seekers are also appreciative of a checklist of potential employers that can be sorted by industry and size of staff.

Access to resources such as these helps level the playing field and enables the small business entrepreneur to be a contender in the competitive commercial marketplace, while enabling the library to remain relevant in today's world.

Major directories include the following:

D&B Total U.S. Million Dollar Database—A Dun & Bradstreet database of over 14 million businesses that provides comprehensive marketing information on all U.S. businesses and a significant segment of Canadian businesses. It allows searching by numerous factors including geographic level, executive title, line of business, SIC or NAICS code, and so on. Fund-raisers often use the executive biographies feature to target college alumni.

Hoover's—A Dun & Bradstreet database with information on over 12 million companies that includes in-depth coverage of 35,00 of the world's top business enterprises.

ReferenceUSA—An InfoUSA database, it covers 15 million U.S. businesses searchable by company, geographic level, sales volume, number of employees, SIC or NAICS code, and owner gender. *ReferenceUSA* also has residential, Canadian, health care, new businesses, new homeowners, and new movers modules. Home improvement firms, security systems companies, and home decorating services frequently peruse these lists.

ThomasNet—www.thomasnet.com—is a free database that provides access to more than 650,000 industrial companies indexed by over 67,000 product and service categories. It also has an international component in 11 languages from 28 countries. A trusted resource for manufacturers and the construction industry, the database provides access to over 67,000 manufacturers, distributors, and service providers. An example of its specificity is its listing of 670,000 suppliers for 229 different types of bolts.

Allbusiness.com is perfect for libraries facing funding difficulties. This website, sponsored by Dun & Bradstreet, gives company profiles for over 14 million U.S. businesses and can be searched or viewed by industry. It contains articles from numerous trade magazines and business journals, as well as a host of other business tools. Extensive material on franchising includes an analysis of the top 300 franchises.

Trade Associations, Publications, and Periodicals

Small Business Sourcebook is a Gale Cengage Learning annual publication with over 27,000 print and online resources designed to facilitate the start-up, development, and growth of specific small businesses. Its resources include periodicals, franchise opportunities, and associations. It is also included online in the Small Business Resource Center.

Business Source Premier—An EBSCO business periodical remote-access database that covers over 3,600 business periodicals, with full-text access to 2,400. Of particular interest to business is the access to SWOT (strengths, weaknesses, opportunities, and threats) analyses of companies provided by Datamonitor. Users can choose to view only certain publications such as industry profiles, market research reports, trade journals, and so on. For example, such trade publications as *Furniture Today, Appliance Manufacturer,* and *Textile World* are often very helpful to sales people and job hunters.

LexisNexis Library Express—This provides access to over 9,500 news, business, and legal sources. It contains deep backfiles and up-to-the-minute stories in national and regional newspapers, wire services, broadcast transcripts, international news, and foreign-language sources.

Marketing Resources

As mentioned previously, primary and some secondary market research is financially out of the reach of the potential entrepreneur and the small business owner. Much of it is also beyond the budget allowance of all but the largest public libraries. Secondary market analyses, however, can provide research findings about marketing, merchandising, and consumer demographics. A number of newsletters and research reports from EPM Communications include *Research Alert, Marketing to Women, Youth Markets Alert,* and *Entertainment Marketing,* which provide synopses of major market research surveys. The Plunkett Research series, another tool for market research, business intelligence, associations and organizations, and industry trends and statistics, covers thirty-two industries, including entertainment and media; e-commerce and Internet; food, beverages, and tobacco; nanotechnology and micro-electro-mechanical systems; and retailing. These almanacs, available online and in print, provide profiles of hundreds of leading companies. The online version allows the export of custom mailing lists and data sets in MS Excel or text files.

Another producer of market research studies, Richard K. Miller & Associates (www.rkma.com), issues a number of annual publications, including *Consumer Behavior, Consumer Health and Wellness, Consumer Marketing, Retail Business Market Research Handbook, Leisure Market Research Handbook,* and *Healthcare Business Market Research Handbook.*

Market Share Reporter, compiled by Gale Cengage Learning, is an annual compilation of reported market share data for over 200 products, commodities, services, and facilities from over 6,400 companies and 3,200 brands arranged by four-digit SIC code. Entries are on such topics as leading online ticket vendors, largest green design firms, growth in DVD software market 2000–2012, leading outsource payroll processors, and top cranberry juice brands.

Special Industry Resources

Often, in particular localities, there are certain industries that have more representation than others, and libraries find they need to identify and collect resources for that industry. In our area, many requests from home renovators, home construction companies, and electrical, masonry, and plumbing concerns alerted us to the need for bid information, cost data, and labor rates. While some data are not available to public libraries, we were able to locate area bid reports from two sources, Reed Construction Data and BidClerk.com.

Long Island Construction Bulletin; New York City and Long Island Civil Engineering Bulletin. These are weekly services reporting on forthcoming construction projects in the planning, bid, and post-bid stages covering status of job, plan availability, size and details, monetary value of the project, and names of key decision makers. Reed Construction publications cover all of the United States and some international projects as well and are available in print and online.

A national online subscription service, Bidclerk.com allows users to search thousands of construction projects. Each listing includes project details such as contact information, project type, building use, status, location, and description. Contractors can locate projects within local markets that meet their exact criteria.

Both our reference and circulating collections have copies of the popular R.S. Means publications, including:

Building Construction Cost Data
Heavy Construction Cost Data
Labor Rates for the Construction Industry
Light Commercial Construction Cost Data
Repair and Remodeling Cost Data
Residential Construction Cost Data
Facilities Construction Cost Data
Interior Home Improvement Cost Data
Exterior Home Improvement Cost Data
Concrete and Masonry Cost Data

And from BNI Building News:

BNI General Construction Costbook
BNI Remodeling Costbook
BNI Home Remodeling Costbook
Architects, Contractors & Engineers (ACE) Guide to Construction Costs

Along with local town and municipal building codes, we have also added a series of New York State building codes, including:

National Electrical Code
Building Code of New York State
Residential Code of New York State
Fire Code of New York State
Mechanical Code of New York State
Plumbing Code of New York State
Property Maintenance Code of New York State
Energy Conservation Construction Code of New York State
Fuel Gas Code of New York State

The General Code—E Code Library—www.generalcode.com/webcode2 .html—provides free access to many local village, town, and municipal codes. Also, many town and village websites have added links to their respective codes.

An excellent group of articles detailing both free and fee-based online sources of construction industry information is *Searcher* magazine's three-part series by Angela Kangiser, which will conclude by the end of 2011. Entitled "The Construction Industry Online," they cover commercial building and construction within both the private and public sectors and residential and green construction.

An online subscription to the Thomson Gale Legal Forms database provides a number of building and construction legal forms, including those for bids, change orders, contracts, covenants, project management, and liens. Both real estate and construction industry people make use of our library's subscription to the RealQuest database (www.Realquest.com) of local property ownership and tax map information. Also, lists of local real estate sales with price and owner/seller data, foreclosure schedules, *lis pendens* or pre-foreclosure notices, and lists of new area businesses are in popular demand.

Both potential and existing business people need to keep current on the condition of their industry. *Standard & Poor's NetAdvantage* subscription includes a semiannual home-building industry report giving valuable key business ratios and statistics, population projections, housing starts rankings of major home builders, median prices, and an extensive commentary on the industry's status. Also included is a multi-page tutorial on "How to Analyze a Homebuilding Company."

To increase public awareness of this collection, our staff has created a bibliography entitled "Materials for the Building and Construction Trades" (figure 2.2).

Legal and Government Resources

The law area that has seen the most interest is the collection of resources devoted to the legal aspects of starting and managing a small business. All libraries can take advantage of the free websites that federal, state, and local governments have set up to assist new businesses. One we have found particularly helpful is www.sba.gov.

The U.S. Small Business Administration (www.sba.gov) is a multi-tiered website covering many aspects of small business. One segment addresses registering a business, and obtaining licenses and permits for certain establishments. For example, if a patron is considering starting a restaurant in zip code 80111 (Englewood, Colorado), entering the business zip code will direct him to the appropriate registration, permit, and license information for that locality.

In addition, the site addresses tax registration, incorporation filings, DBAs (doing business as names), and employer and insurance requirements. Links also connect to each state's particulars for starting and operating a business, training and assistance, and city, county, and municipality business guidance.

As prospective business owners weigh the advantages of one form of business entity over another or business owners need to know how to save a business, we have discovered that they have found the titles from the Nolo Press in California and the Nova Publishing Company in Carbondale, Illinois, to be very useful. Resources include the following:

From Nolo:

Incorporate Your Business
Federal Employment Law
Bankruptcy for Small Business Owners
Profit from Your Idea
The Partnership Book
Save Your Small Business

FIGURE 2.2 Increase public awareness of a specific collection with a bibliography brochure.

Women's Small Business Kit: A Step-by-Step Legal Guide
Every Nonprofit's Tax Guide
Your Limited Liability Corporation
Legal Forms for Starting & Running a Small Business
Corporate Records Handbook
Working for Yourself: Law & Taxes for Independent Contractors,
     Freelancers & Consultants
From Nova:
Limited Liability Company: Small Business Start-Up Kit
Partnership: Small Business Start-Up Kit
S-Corporation: Small Business Start-Up Kit
Sole Proprietorship: Small Business Start-Up Kit
Corporation: Small Business Start-Up Kit
Small Business Legal Forms Simplified

While the Miller Business Resource Center's law collection now includes a Westlaw subscription to New York and federal laws and cases, the print versions of *McKinney's Consolidated Laws of New York,* the *United States Code Annotated,* and the *Supreme Court Reporter* have been retained. Both patrons and librarians are more familiar with them.

Business librarians assisting human resource professionals find pertinent information in the following:

Employee Compensation. Business & Legal Reports
Family and Medical Leave Guide. Commerce Clearing House.
U.S. Master Employee Benefits Guide. Commerce Clearing House.

International Business

While the Miller Business Resource Center always owned basic importing and exporting directories and guides, when the business librarians started to attend the HIA's International Trade Committee meetings, they began to investigate acquiring other internationally focused materials. At one committee meeting they attended, the HIA members explained that they had been working on a project—a guide to assistance for the international business traveler. The librarians offered to compile a bibliography of available websites. From that moment on, the librarians have been regular members of the group; together they produced and published *The Road Warrior Guide for Business Travelers,* which was distributed to the HIA membership and at the HIA Annual Trade Show. This publication firmed up an already developing egalitarian relationship between the library's Miller Business Resource Center and the business community. It clearly established the library as a vital resource and distinguished the librarians as information specialists.

The Miller Business Resource Center has also continued to update its resources on business etiquette, both for domestic and international business. A recent bibliography, *Business Etiquette for the Global Environment,* annotates the Miller Business Resource Center's current resources on the topic. In addition, the center subscribes to *World Trade Reference,* an online remote-access reference source from World Trade Press giving definitions and translations of trade terms, basics of world trade, information on world tariffs and taxes, international payments, major trading countries, import/export documentation, and a searchable database of customs rulings.

Not-for-Profits

First-time fund-raising organizations often find the prospects for success daunting. Luckily, there are an increasing number of resources to help the nonprofit corporation. The Miller Business Resource Center was the recipient of two not-for-profit collections: one from the Association of Fund Raising Professionals and the other the gift of the Enterprise Foundation. Both consist of circulating nonprofit pamphlets, monographs, and videos on major topics such as fund-raising basics, board governance, and effective programming. In addition, the library subscribes to the *Foundation Directory Online,* which provides patrons with information on U.S. grantmakers and their grants, pertinent websites, and grant-writing tools. A circulating collection of fund-raising guidebooks, nonprofit corporation start-up guides, and grant proposal-writing handbooks complements these resources.

Circulating and Periodical Materials

To assist prospective small business entrepreneurs, the circulating collection of start-up guides from publishers such as Entrepreneur and Self-Counsel are popular items. Recent titles include:

Entrepreneur Press

Start Your Own Blogging Business
Start Your Own Freelance and Copywriting Business
Start Your Own Medical Claims Billing Service
Start Your Own Pet Business and More

Self-Counsel Press

Start & Run a Retail Business
Start & Run a Bookkeeping Business
Start & Run a Coffee Bar

Major areas of business research such as investment, banking, business management, franchises, not-for profit organizations, and home businesses can locate materials in the Miller Business Resource Center's periodical collection. Newspapers include:

New York Times
Wall Street Journal
Wall Street Transcript
Financial Times
Investors Business Daily
New York Law Journal
Long Island Business News
Crain's New York Business

Business marketers who are searching for the top local companies find the annual editions of *Long Island Business News Book of Lists* and *Crain's New York Business Book of Lists* extremely helpful. The top private and public companies are profiled, as well as the leading companies in many industries. Crain Communications also publishes a *Book of Lists* for Chicago, Cleveland, and Detroit.

To market our collection of new business books, we have found it a good practice to display a copy of the *Wall Street Journal's* weekly column of best business books as well as the *New York Times* monthly business best sellers list in our new business books section. Library copies of the lists' items are available for circulation from these shelves. Also located in this unit are new career materials, current start-up business guides, and marketing and sales handbooks. The new book unit has good display surfaces as well as shelves, and business patrons tend to gravitate toward this eye-catching unit. The display items need constant changing because patrons keep checking items out.

Traditionally, the reference librarian or librarians are stationed at the reference desk. When we started to envision the Miller Business Resource Center, we experimented with having a librarian at a desk in the business and career collections area. It was amazing how many people were wandering around hoping to find something to help them with a job search, new business idea, marketing or management problem, or a college choice. When the library renovation was completed and the Miller Business Resource Center was officially inaugurated, a business reference desk was placed front and center. Patrons truly appreciate the assistance of a trained business librarian. Over and over again, we hear patrons' expressions of satisfaction. Librarians who know their services and collections and who listen and analyze patrons' requests are vital to any public library business service.

In increasing numbers, patrons are coming to libraries searching for resume help, interviewing skills, and small business assistance. Building business and career collections requires both time and money. But if libraries are willing to invest in the collections and services that their patrons can use to develop their job skills and expand their businesses through better marketing and sales techniques, the return can be not only an expansion of local economic activity but also a recognition of the importance and relevance of the library to the community.

Finding Jobs and Creating Career Paths

At last count, over 14 million U.S. workers were unemployed. For many, unemployment benefits will soon end; for others, they already have. All are considering their options.

> Should I change fields? Should I open my own business? Do I need more training?
>
> How do I write a resume? What am I really interested in doing? Am I too old to get a job?
>
> What do I say at a job interview and what do I not say?

Many job seekers have come to libraries to find answers and seek help. Media reports detail the influx of patrons filling libraries that are, themselves, facing budgetary constraints. "With unemployment rising, people are flocking to the library for help finding jobs, switching careers, brushing up resumes, or checking the financial ratings of companies that are advertising for help" (*New York Times*, March 15, 2009).

A *New York Times* article from April 2, 2009, related the efforts of the Arlington Heights Memorial Library in suburban Chicago that, in trying "to anticipate the new needs of its neighborhood, . . . has created a job-search desk, and it has recruited volunteer professionals to review resumes, set up a support and networking group for the unemployed, and assembled a Web site offering the best of its online resources."

An ALA news release announcing the organization's annual *State of America's Libraries* report cites job-related activities as a priority use of library computers and Internet services. And "libraries are offering programs tailored to meet local community economic needs, providing residents with guidance (including sessions with career advisers), training and workshops in resume writing and interviewing, job-search resources, and connections with outside agencies that offer training and job placement." In all, 58 percent of urban libraries, 66 percent of suburban libraries, and 61 percent of rural libraries provide services for job seekers.

In looking at websites and speaking with librarians across the country, we have tried to examine the proactive approaches public libraries have taken to address the job crisis. The following highlights actions libraries have been undertaking. Can an individual library do all of them? Probably not. However, it is very probable that at least some of them could be effective in your library. Reviewing the list and the accounts that follow will also reveal how starting a project often can generate funds that can help continue it or start a new one.

Career Resources at Public Libraries

Website Links and In-Print Resources

annotated lists of new career acquisitions

announcements of local job fairs (in print and on websites)

announcements of upcoming programs and workshops

announcements of civil service tests

career blogs

civil service test applications

featured career resources

interactive career test links

links to assessment tools and career exploration sites

links to internships and volunteer opportunities

links to unemployment resources

links to local employment agencies and executive recruiters

local job listings

online application tutorials, assistance, and workshops

Resume Maker on all library public computers

resume review

salary guides

Job-Promoting Activities

assistance with unemployment claims

career and business databases

career counseling and coaching

civil service test guides

collaborative partnerships with other career agencies and libraries

computer classes

enhance job-seeking print and online resources in collections

featured career speaker series

hosting job fairs (in collaboration with Department of Labor)
interview clinic
job clubs and networking groups
mobile job centers
proctoring services
sample business plans for new businesses
SAT and PSAT test preparation classes
seminars and workshops
Train the Trainer workshops for librarians
WiFi access

It is surely a "sign of the times" that many of the job workshops presently being offered in public libraries center around the topic "Finding a New Career after Fifty." Every careers librarian we have spoken with has mentioned that an increasing number of people who are seeking career assistance are over fifty years old, and unemployment is totally new to most of them. Most have never written a resume or a cover letter. Many of these people are also unfamiliar with and intimidated by the computer. The lack of computer skills is a huge obstacle in a world where even McDonald's requires an online application.

Almost two years ago, observing the trepidation and sense of urgency in many recently unemployed patrons, Tonya Badillo, a librarian at the Long Branch Free Public Library in Long Branch, New Jersey, developed a Virtual Career Center for the library's website. Noting that many patrons had very limited computer skills and had difficulty with the major employment websites, she included a section offering online tutorials on basic and advanced computer skills such as "Using the Mouse and the Keyboard, "Internet, Email and WiFi Basics," and "Windows and Microsoft Applications." She also concentrated more on local job assistance, career exploration, specific career finders, interviews and resume building, and college information.

Another segment of the site features resources for:

Additional Diversity Resources
African American Resources
Back to Work Resources
Disabilities and the Workplace

Ex-Offenders Job Resources

Latin/Hispanic Resources
Nonprofit Resources
Self-Employment Resources
Seniors in the Workplace
Teen/Student Employment
Women's Resources
Working Parent Resources

The New Jersey State Library asked to post the Virtual Career Center on its website, and Long Branch has made the template available to all libraries. The success of this project led to a grant to the Long Branch Free Public Library from the New Jersey State Library which has provided funding for the library to revamp its computer lab with new technology and to develop and offer ten-week "Back to Work" courses covering all phases of the job search and employment process. The grant also enabled the library to hire a human resources trainer to teach the courses. Long Branch is now concentrating on a new course preparing ex-offenders to reenter the work force.

Badillo was thrilled when 80 percent of the first enrollees of the Back to Work class returned to the library to report success at finding a job!

Filling out an online application can be extremely frustrating for those who lack computer skills and who are experiencing unemployment for the first time in many years. In response to this problem, the Newton Free Library in Newton, Massachusetts, holds a workshop twice a month to assist people with online applications. Patrons can take the course as many times as they wish. The library has put the handouts, training syllabus, and PowerPoint presentation online for anyone who wishes to use it. The library also has an ongoing "Job Series" of free programs presented by local professionals focusing on various job search aspects. Program titles have included:

Help! I Haven't Looked for a Job in Years! Tips for Navigating Today's Job Market
Managing Your Finances between Jobs
Interviews, Networking, and Career Conversations: What Do I Say?
What's Next? Focusing on Your Strengths
Networking: Successful Approaches for Job Seekers and All Professionals

Are You Linked In? Using Social Media to Make Career Connections
Communication Tools for Work and Personal Relationships: It's Not
about Talking

In addition, the library also maintains a Quick Job Blog Search. The purpose of the blog is to post websites, blogs, and articles that will help facilitate Internet job searching. Subjects have included:

Tips for Getting, Finding and Keeping a Job
Why Is It So Hard to Apply for a Job through a Company's Website?
What Companies Are Laying Off or Hiring?

The blog also contains postings of career services in other Massachusetts Minuteman libraries. For example, it alerted patrons to a six-week "Jump-Start Your Job Search" workshop that was given at the Waltham Public Library in Waltham, Massachusetts, that covered not only the job search process but also the feelings associated with being unemployed. At the completion of the course, as described by Laura Bernheim, head of reference services, the class members formed the nucleus of Job Notes, a weekly meeting of job seekers who get together at the library to share ideas, discuss programs, and lend support.

The library has also partnered with the Massachusetts One-Stop Career Center; the One-Stop refers clients to the library's program, and the library sends patrons to the One-Stop for career counseling.

Librarians are also developing "Train the Trainer" workshops to advise other librarians on locating available resources in assisting job search patrons. For the last two years Deb Weltsch, jobs librarian at the Poughkeepsie Public Library, has conducted a series of workshops for librarians in the mid-Hudson area of New York State. Entitled "One-on-One Immediate Job Help/Referrals" and "Aid and Resources for Job Seekers," the workshops explored such topics as:

federal benefits programs
unemployment benefits
resources for Spanish-speaking patrons
community college counseling centers
job training and preparation for licensed or certified occupations

Job Corps
civil service resources
job search banks' sites and job banks
resume services and guides
how to help patrons with resume formatting
identifying potential employers
"Best Bet" databases

The Central Library of the Buffalo and Erie County Public Library in Buffalo, New York, is located just doors away from the Buffalo Employment & Training Center (BETC), the Department of Labor's "One Stop" career center for the area. In partnership with the One-Stop, Kara Stock, jobs librarian, conducts quarterly workshops at BETC for job seekers on the use of the library's databases such as *LearningExpress, Gale's Business and Company Resource Database, ReferenceUSA,* and EBSCO's *Career Library* in building skills and locating job opportunities. Stock also gives the workshop, on an annual basis, to local job networking groups and has recently begun presenting it at local job fairs in the Buffalo area.

The library's Career Resources web page, which Stock maintains for all thirty-seven system libraries, provides links to local, state, and federal civil service jobs and test preparation, local career counseling career centers (both free and for fee), as well as resume, cover letter, and interview guides. The Buffalo and Erie County Library has also installed Resume Maker software on all the library's public computers.

The opening web page of the Skokie Public Library's Employment Resource Center offers a list of resources for individuals including " Individual Orientation to the Employment Resource Center." That alone makes it special! Even though almost all libraries try to give a patron a personal introduction to their services and collections, we often forget to offer it on our website, and patrons still approach us with "I'm sorry to bother you but. . . ." Tours of the Employment Resource Center, which provides training in using the library and the Internet for a job search, lectures on employment topics, Internet presentations, and meeting room space, are also offered to local groups and community agencies.

The Skokie Public Library has partnered with Jewish Vocational Services, which has provided two career counselors twice a month plus a moderator for the Skokie Career Support Group which meets once a month at the library. Michael Buhmann, Skokie Library career specialist, explained that the support group, which gathers together between 25 and 50 members per meeting, worked out very well, with job seekers helping each other and offering mutual emotional support. Buhmann, who attends each meeting, said he found it beneficial for him, as a librarian, because he learned from attendees about different career websites and local hiring opportunities for patrons.

In partnership with the Chamber of Commerce, the library holds two career fairs each year, which draw an audience of over 150 attendees and enable job seekers to attend a variety of employment topic seminars.

Programs demonstrating the unique applications for local businesses and careers of the new Skokie Library Digital Media Lab are on the drawing board for the library's near future.

Some public library career centers have long-established histories. Many were started in the 1980s to meet the job needs of homemakers returning to the workforce. Now, all find their focus shifting. Instead of patrons contemplating leaving a secure job for a more challenging position in a new company or a career change to an entirely new field, the priority for most clients is simply finding a job.

Since 1976, the Career Center of the Cuyahoga Public Library, located in the Maple Heights Branch, has been assisting patrons with career and education planning. Four full-time career counselors are available to help patrons with job search strategies, resume and cover letter preparation, and coaching for a job interview. A counselor will also review a patron's resume and cover letter sent by e-mail or dropped off at the library.

Career counselors also facilitate several weekday job clubs and networking groups in Maple Heights and other branches. These clubs, open to all who are out of work or changing careers, offer support and networking opportunities with job tips. All career counselors are certified/licensed counselors, and the director of the Career Center is Librarian Bonnie Easton.

Career workshops held in numerous library branches in spring 2010 offered the following seminars:

Behavior-Based Interviewing
Career Planning
Creating Cover Letters

Creating Resumes with Optimal Resume
Internet Job Search
LinkedIn 101
Online Job Applications
Over 50 and Out of Work
Resume Tips and Trends
Social Networking and Your Job Search

Popular and successful, the counselors see approximately 1,800 persons per year, and job club attendance averages from 30 to 40 persons per session. Workshops, which are often given in four branches for each topic, are always filled to capacity.

The library has also created an extensive online "Survival Guide," a referral source for those facing unemployment and underemployment in the greater Cleveland area. It is a compilation of agencies offering career counseling, job search instruction, placement and training, legal and financial assistance, and special services to people with disabilities and veterans.

Also in operation for over thirty years is the WEBS Program, a free career and educational counseling service of the Westchester Library System in Westchester County, New York. Directed by Elaine Sozzi and staffed by professionals with graduate degrees in counseling, WEBS has successfully served over 30,000 clients since 1980 through seminars, workshops, and counseling. In partnership with the Westchester Career Counselors Network, WEBS conducts two eight-week courses five times a year in five or six large Westchester library branches. Managing Your Career in Changing Times, a career development seminar, helps patrons evaluate their skills and interests, use online career information, learn effective job strategies, explore occupational alternatives, and examine educational training available in Westchester County. A second course, Take Charge! Career/Life Planning after 50, a life planning seminar, helps people explore new ways of working in a high-tech world and also provides a clear direction for the next stage of their career. Both these courses are preceded by two-week introduction sessions where students take assessment tests such as the Myers-Briggs or the Strong Interest Inventory to help determine their interests and abilities.

In June 2009 the H&R Block Business and Career Center opened at the Kansas City Public Library. The H&R Block Foundation, which is headquartered in Kansas City, Missouri, provided a $600,000 grant for the library to develop a 2,800-square-foot business center that would focus on small business and entrepreneurship. As the center was being built, it was decided, with the current economic climate, that careers should be the main focus area.

The business center is staffed by three full-time librarians, and patrons can make appointments with them to discuss their business or career needs. A collection of print and electronic resources focuses on small business, entrepreneurship, career information, not-for-profits, and grant research. Especially designed for job seekers and people who are exploring new careers, the Vault Online Career Library contains videos on specific occupations as well as information on education, training, and required certifications.

Career programs include Job Search Communications: Cover Letters, E-mail, and Phone Follow-Up, Interviewing: Prepare to Dazzle, and Career Teens. The library also offers a twice-weekly GED course.

To market their business and career programs, the staff of the H&R Block Center has reached out to the following community groups: Women's Employment Network, United Way, Good Will, and Beyond the Conviction.

Pamela Jenkins, manager of the center and business librarian for the Kansas City Public Library, is currently developing a survey to poll the success rate of the job seekers that have been assisted by the center.

In September 2009 the New York Public Library's (NYPL's) Science, Industry and Business Library (SIBL) responded to the employment crisis by creating Job Search Central as a "one-stop shop for job seekers." Provided are an extensive program of job-related classes and job events; career coaching sessions, provided free by appointment; remote access to career databases for NYPL cardholders; small business counseling from SCORE (Service Corps of Retired Executives); and access to an exhaustive list of links to job boards and employment services, as well as PDFs of career guides and resources.

Classes include:

Communicate with Confidence
Coping with Job Loss
Job Seekers: Download a Customized Company List for Contacts
Pink Slips: How Losing Your Job Can Be a Good Thing
The Power of Networking
Resume Renovation

Dealing with the Stress of an Extended Job Search
Interviewing Skills

PDF guides include:

Job Search Tips from the NYPL
How to Begin Your Job Search
How to Write a Resume
How to Prepare for an Interview
Career and Job Resources for On-Site Use
Rights and Benefits Information: A SIBL Source Guide

We had the privilege of speaking with Bernice Kao, who has developed the award-winning Fresno County Public Library Career Center in Fresno, California, and is responsible for job services, including collections and programs, at the library's thirty-seven branches. An accomplished motivational speaker, Kao has addressed professional conferences at state, national, and international levels. For over three years, she has conducted two free job clinics, each held monthly at the library. The Resume Makeover clinic is open to all as Kao offers advice to repair, renew, and revitalize a job seeker's resume. The class focuses on the pros and cons of many types of resumes, and the correct resume format for a particular job that will make the applicant stand out. To those who have written or revised their resumes after following the guidelines of Kao's "Ingredients of an Effective Resume" (figure 2.3), she offers e-mail resume review. The Interview Clinic encourages job seekers to practice their interviews with Kao for advice and coaching before their next employment interview. Kao believes that outreach to government agencies, nonprofit organizations, and the local business community is the key to effective and innovative library service. Kao has recently added a third monthly workshop, a Job Search Clinic, which focuses on starting a job search and incorporates elements of the other two.

Since its inception at the Middle Country Public Library as a State University of New York (SUNY) grant program in the 1980s, the Career Information Center has been an integral part of our pattern of library service. Because it was such a popular service, the library decided to continue it on a permanent basis. Our part-time career counselors all have master's degrees in counseling or business and assist patrons in 45-minute one-on-one sessions on three

INGREDIENTS OF AN EFFECTIVE RESUME

Summary of Qualifications

These should match what the current position requires. Five popular areas that most positions like to focus on are

- Customer Services
- Management Skills
- Leadership/Training Experiences
- Computer Technology
- Applicable Language Skills

Work History/Experiences

Include your previous job titles, company/organization names, places, and years that you worked there in reverse chronological order. Don't bother with months; and limit history to the last 10 years. Candidates who describe their past work history in great detail are people who show their laundry list. This kind of resume will invite most hiring agencies to drop it from any further contact—telephone inquiry/personal interview.

Education History

Include Degree/s, Schools, and Years. You may list any relevant continuing education courses/seminars that may add value to this new position. Important certificates that you earned should be listed here with the Name, Place, and Year.

Scholarship and Awards

List the industry-specific and relevant ones that you were awarded, including Award Type, Institutional Source, and Years.

Community Services and Volunteering Work

This is very important for applying a job at either a regular company, government agency, or a non-profit organization. Almost every industry nowadays considers community involvement an essential part of running a sound business. Your Boy Scout/Girl Scout activities and civic fund-raising chairmanship may be way back, but they still count!

References upon Request

Bring two copies of your three references to every interview with names and phone numbers only. Their addresses and relationships with you are not necessary.

It is in the first *seven seconds* that a busy human resources professional peruses your resume. If that person doesn't find anything from the Summary of Qualifications impressive, he/she won't go on, thus your resume will not land on the To Call Pile for a telephone interview.

A resume with no more than three fonts on one page is easier to read. You need to leave plenty of white space on the right side for interviewers to write notes about you.

Reprinted by permission of Bernice Kao, Career Coach, Fresno County Library.

FIGURE 2.3   Job services clinics, such as Bernice Kao's Resume Makeover Clinic at Fresno County Library, are a natural fit with business reference.

evenings, two weekdays, and Saturdays. Career counselors follow a variety of procedures, depending on the patron's needs, including the following:

- For patrons attempting to pinpoint a career direction or deciding to change careers, the counselors administer the Strong Interest Inventory or Myers-Briggs questionnaire. Answers are tabulated and the patron returns for a second interview to discuss the results and possible career paths.
- College-bound students and often one or two parents come to discuss college choices, the application process, the application essay, interviews, scholarships, and loans. Once a year, a librarian and a career counselor introduce the library's special services at an "after graduation" program at the two district high schools.
- High school graduating seniors not planning to attend college often make counseling appointments to discuss apprenticeships, technical school choices, or military service.
- Job-seeking patrons may request assistance on writing a resume, developing cover letters, job interview techniques, and follow-up procedures.
- Recently, a new outreach service has met with instant success. The Saturday career counselor spends one and a half hours on the main library floor answering questions from the public at large. In addition to helping people with their job or college searches, this outreach has publicized the career service and encouraged patrons to make counseling appointments.

The Miller Business Resource Center houses a collection of over 3,000 test books. While the majority are for preparing for civil service and other occupation-related exams, the latest SAT, GRE, GMAT, LSAT, and other educational guides and handbooks are included as well. While this collection is restricted to Middle Country Public Library card-holding patrons, we maintain a Ready Reference Pending Civil Service Test Book Area for out-of-district patrons to use in the library. We always have civil service test application forms available, along with job announcements from local businesses and the local university, SUNY at Stony Brook.

In addition to multiple copies of the very popular *Occupational Outlook Handbook* and the latest edition of the classic *What Color Is Your Parachute?* an extensive collection of career books describes occupations from actuary to zookeeper. An additional 400 titles explore resume writing, cover letters, and the employment interview.

In addition, in the 1980s the MCPL began the development of the *Community Resource Database,* a comprehensive information and referral resource, via telephone, and now Internet, for human services on Long Island. Although the database is still managed by the library, it has now been incorporated into the *2-1-1 Long Island Database.* Part of this database provides information on all adult continuing education and certificate programs offered by the more than twenty public and private colleges and universities and public technical schools on Long Island. Persons seeking a local certificate program for a career in information technology, personal fitness, environmental management, or as a paralegal or drug counselor can access the program via the database.

Resources for Starting a Career Service

Even if there are limited funds, public libraries can provide access to a host of free career services on their websites. Most career web pages provide links to the following resources.

CareerOneStop, sponsored by the Education and Training Administration of the U.S. Department of Labor, is a portal site with links to assessing skills, abilities, and work values, exploring career options, updating skills, preparing resumes and cover letters, and finding education and training. The career services locator at www.servicelocator.org provides the locations of over 1,800 comprehensive and 1,100 affiliate One-Stop career centers nationwide, as well as job banks in all fifty states.

O*Net Online, accessible from the CareerOneStop site, is part of the Occupational Information Network that has replaced the no longer published *Dictionary of Occupational Titles.* With this source, a user can browse groups of similar occupations to explore careers or focus on occupations that use a specific tool or software.

In addition, basic federal resources such as the latest edition of the *Occupational Outlook Handbook* and *Career Guide to Industries* are now available full text in electronic format at www.bls.gov/OOH and www.bls.gov/OOH/cg. Both of these sources detail training and education needed, earnings, expected job prospects, job descriptions, and working conditions for many different types of jobs and occupations in various industries, as well as providing job search tips and information about the job market in specific geographic areas.

Career Builder—This contains nationwide job listings searchable by industry, company, type, and location, and allows resume posting.

Career Journal—A *Wall Street Journal* site, it has a resume writing and posting service, employment news, career videos, and job searching capabilities.

Indeed.com—A major job search engine for job boards, job sites, blogs, newspapers, professional association listings, and company career pages.

Monster.com—Browse career snapshots of 2,500 occupations, post a resume, search job listings, and get advice on job strategy, interviewing, and career development.

Riley's Internet Job Guide—A directory of employment opportunities and career information sources and services including information on resumes and cover letters, self-assessment resources, networking, job fairs, and support groups.

Susan Ireland Resumes—This provides writing tips, sample resumes, cover letters, thank-you notes, job interview tips and questions, and salary negotiation skills. There is a "career option" section with salary and growth forecast information and suitability for part-time work information. The site is also available in Spanish.

WorkSearch—Sponsored by the AARP Foundation, WorkSearch is a customized online system that helps qualified individuals age forty and over to assess their skills, match to careers, and link to training and job openings. It also provides virtual job search coaching and job-seeking techniques and resources.

The AARP has also launched a new online job search engine to serve workers age fifty and older. With more than one million listings, seniors can identify openings by specifying criteria such as state, zip code, industry, occupation, and job title (*AARP Bulletin*, November 2010). The site also has webinars for job seekers, sample elevator speeches (i.e., a short self-description of who a person is and what he or she does), announcements of seasonal jobs for retirees, and best employers for workers over fifty.

If your community has a large number of retirees or workers over fifty who might be looking for work, the site at http://jobs.aarp.org would be a good website to link to.

The subscription databases that we found were most often used by public library career centers include the following ones.

Resume Tools

Resume Maker—This provides over 1,200 professionally written sample resumes. Cover letter examples, job interview practice questions, salary negotiation information, and resume posting and job search tools are included.

OptimalResume—This includes sample resumes and cover letters, an interview preparation program, a video resume component, skills assessment tools, and links to O*Net Online.

Job Search and Testing Tools

Career Cruising—www.careercruising.com—An online career guidance and planning system that provides hundreds of career profiles, each containing two multimedia interviews; an interest assessment test with a skills assessment; a personal portfolio tool with a built-in resume builder; and a resource of "how-to's" for career advisors, counselors, and teachers.

EBSCO's Career Library—www.ebsco.com—This provides information on over 2,500 occupations, "Cool Jobs," and post-secondary career paths. Includes an occupation video library in both English and Spanish, surveys and assessments based on sixteen federal career clusters, and sample GED, ACT/SAT, and proficiency tests.

Ferguson's Career Guidance Center—www.fofweb.com—is divided into three main sections: jobs, skills, and resources. The jobs section contains information on over 3,300 jobs and 94 industries. The skills section offers advice on job applications, interview success, and work environment behavior and includes 90 sample resumes and cover letters. The resources section includes information on career assessment features, the school search, scholarships, internships, fellowships, and organizations, as well as 290 videos on jobs, industries, and career development skills.

LearningExpress Library Database—www.learnatest.com—The Job Search and Workplace Skills Learning Center assists in resume crafting, strengthening job searches, and interviewing and networking skills, and it has job postings. It includes 300 practice tests (GED preparation, U.S. citizenship, electrical, plumbing, air traffic control, etc.) and e-books to prepare for civil service, education, and allied health career tests.

Testing and Education Reference Center with Careers—www.gale.cengage .com/TestingAndEducation/quick.htm—This contains over 100 practice exams for career tests (NCLEX, ASVAB, PRAXIS, civil service, and military), college prep, and high school. With the Virtual Career Library, individual modules will assist in preparing resumes, writing cover letters, preparing for interviews, negotiating salary considerations, and developing networking skills.

Tutor.com-Career Center—Designed for libraries serving small to medium populations, this has resources for job seekers and adult learners in conducting a job search, preparing for the GED, or going back to school. It includes resume templates, local job openings, academic work sheets, and standardized test samples. It provides real-time help from online career experts on writing resumes or cover letters and polishing business letters or proposals.

Libraries are also referring their job-seeking patrons to their business databases such as *ReferenceUSA, D&B Total U.S. Million Dollar Database,* and *Hoover's* (profiled earlier in this chapter) to download lists of prospective employers and company executives and sort them by area, industry, sales, and so on. Databases such as *First Industry, Standard & Poor's NetAdvantage, Plunkett Research, Ltd.,* and *Gale Business and Company Resource Center* are recommended to research industry surveys and trends.

3

Programming

Opening the Doors

With a core business collection on the shelves and new partners in the business community, programming is the next step to a successful business center. Programming is a key component in the success of any public library and it is also integral to the success of a library's business center. A current and relevant collection alone is not enough to get people into even the best business center. A library's business center must offer programming that will attract an even more diverse group of business people.

While you may be comfortable and familiar with programming for the general public, programming for the business community presents different challenges. Many of the business programs offered may appeal to the general public, but they must be planned with the needs of the business community in mind.

Business people are pulled in many directions at work and by other business organizations. They must be convinced that a library program is a good use of their time. Be sure to pick topics that are timely and interesting to the local business community. As you are forming your business center and meeting the local community, ask what they are looking for in terms of programming.

What are the patrons talking about or asking for? Do marketing books have the highest circulation? Are networking books in high demand? As we've mentioned before, talking to the patrons of your business center is important for determining the direction of the center. This is also true for programming. Patrons will be the best guides as to what type of programming should be offered. It is crucial to program success to choose programs that match the interests and needs of the patrons.

As with all programming, it is important to consider your audience when setting program times. Always keep in mind the meeting times and dates of local business organizations. For example, if you know the local Chamber of Commerce meets every Thursday at 9:00 a.m., you should avoid programming at that time.

It is sometimes best to run programs outside of regular business hours. Early morning meetings work for many businesspeople. The Miller Business Resource Center offers a lot of programming at 8:00 a.m. on weekdays. These programs generally end by 10:00 a.m., and the attendees appreciate the opportunity to get back to the office and back to work. While we sometimes offer afternoon and evening programs, the morning sessions work for a majority of the businesses we help. Still, we recognize that these times may not be ideal for all libraries or all programs. It is important to find out what works best for your area. For instance, the Glendale Public Library in Arizona hosts some successful business programs on Saturdays. In California, the Riverside Public Library offers many programs at 6:00 p.m. on weeknights.

Business partners are an excellent source of speakers, panelists, and program leaders. Most have programs that they run throughout the year. Often these organizations host programs in their own facilities and are willing to provide the program at off-site locations, including your business center. Offering partners your space and resources is another way to grow the partnership. Getting them into your center really helps them see what you can offer their clients. Partners may also market the program to groups with which you have not yet formed a relationship. This can help bring additional business patrons to the program and to your library.

Budget concerns can affect how you program in all departments of your library. Keep in mind that while your library may pay for much of the programming offered to the general public, it is not always necessary to pay for your business programming. In fact, you can often host programs that cost little or no money.

Many local government and not-for-profit organizations will provide programming for little or no cost. Contact any local agencies and organizations that work with businesses and inquire about possible programs. Most departments of labor host job fairs; encourage them to host the next one at your library. Your local Small Business Administration office offers lots of programming for small businesses and entrepreneurs. Work with them to offer these programs in your business center. Be sure to show the SBA counselors what your center can offer them and their clients.

Your local business partners are also a good source of free or low-cost programming, although it can be a little trickier to set up. It is important not to host programs that turn into sales pitches for outside products or services. The Miller Business Resource Center has offered programs that have been led by banks, professional organizers, life coaches, public relations specialists, and more. We have always approached these programs as topical and insist that the speaker's product or service not be mentioned or pitched. We do allow speakers to hand out business cards or brochures to audience members who request them. Check your library policy to see how you should handle these types of programs. Teaming with business partners can have many benefits for your business center by allowing you to offer relevant programming and by strengthening your relationship with the businesses with whom you network.

Publishers are another great source for programming. Many publishers have local sales reps. Utilizing these local sales reps for programming can benefit the library in many ways. Databases are an important part of any business library collection, yet many business people may not know the scope of the information offered. A database's worth can be measured by its use. As librarians, we know that we have spent hours and hours figuring out what the best books, encyclopedias, periodicals, and databases would be for the business library; but if the patrons do not use these resources, they are worthless. Contact your local sales rep and encourage him to visit your library for database training. Understanding the scope of the databases offered will ensure their use by the businesses your center helps.

Networking among attendees is an important component of our business programs. Generally, the Miller Business Resource Center's programming includes some time for networking. Coffee and tea are served at the start of the program to encourage conversation among attendees. The Center's librarians also take this time to talk with attendees they know and meet those they don't. It's a great time to introduce new programs and resources.

The way you set up your program space also encourages networking. Rather than just having rows of chairs facing a speaker, arrange the space so it encourages discussion. Our programs often include tables and chairs arranged in an arc around the front of the room. The tables give attendees a place for their beverages and an easy way to take notes. It also allows them to chat with the other people at their table (figure 3.1).

Program Ideas and Some Success Stories

An ideal program for every library business center is an introduction to the center itself along with all of the resources it offers local businesses. This program is a great way to meet your target audience and market your business center.

The Miller Business Resource Center hosts an open house several times a year. This program is a casual introduction to the offerings of the business center. Attendees have the opportunity to browse the center and meet the business librarians. This relaxed atmosphere enables us one-on-one time to find out more about individual businesses and what they hope to get from the center. We also use this time to highlight new resources and technologies, such as business books available for e-readers or MP3 players.

The online business resources of the Miller Business Resource Center are called BIZLINK. The Introduction to BIZLINK program is also offered to our patrons and partners on a regular basis. Because this program is given by our librarians, we can plan and offer it more often than our collaborative programs.

Terry Zarsky, business services librarian from the Pikes Peak Library District (PPLD) in Colorado Springs, Colorado, began the Minding Your Business program over ten years ago to save herself time. After spending hours with individual patrons introducing the business resources available at the PPLD, Zarsky decided to turn it into a program.

Minding Your Business teaches the resources available for PPLD users as well as free Internet sites for businesspeople. The program is aimed at "people who are starting a business or writing a business plan, but it has been adapted at times to focus on the jobseeker as needed." Running twice a month for most of the year, the attendees of Minding Your Business include business owners, people thinking about starting a business, and businesspeople in sales or marketing positions. Zarsky markets this program through flyers at the library and the library's website and blog, as well as her network of business

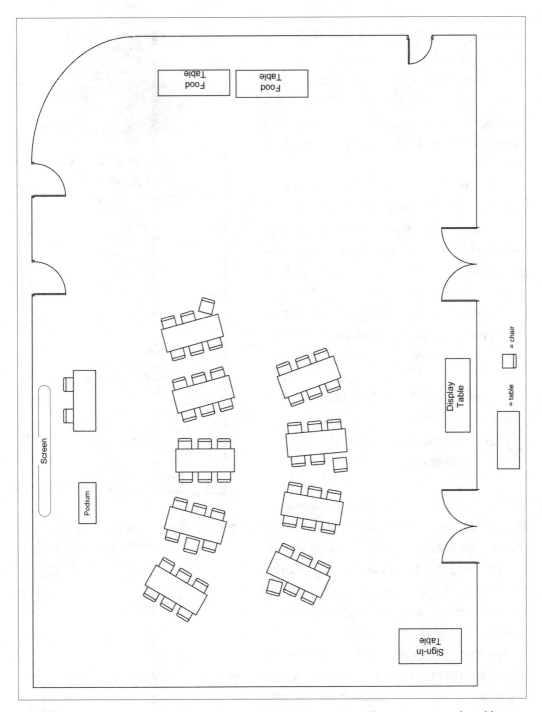

FIGURE 3.1 Using tables in your program space promotes networking. Arranging the tables in an arc encourages discussion among the tables.

groups, including SCORE and the Small Business Development Center.

Minding Your Business is free. Its only costs are Zarsky's time and the cost of a few handouts. This makes it an ideal first program for any new business center (figure 3.2).

Programs for aspiring entrepreneurs are generally very popular. Many people are interested in having their own business but don't know where to start. A series of programs on starting a business can help aspiring entrepreneurs learn about regulatory requirements, start-up loans, business plans, basic marketing, and more. Possible program topics are:

>How to Start Your Own Business
>How to Write a Business Plan
>Hiring Your First Employee
>Small Business Finances

Your partners can be a great resource for these programs. Most local Small Business Development Centers offer these programs to their own clients and are willing to offer them at your locations. (For a full list of these centers, go to www.sba.gov/aboutsba/sbaprograms/sbdc/.)

Another programming resource for aspiring entrepreneurs is the actual businesspeople your center helps. Having a patron with a successful business tell her story can be a great motivator for other patrons starting a business.

In July 2008, the Brooklyn Public Library's Business Library teamed up with the Small Business Development Center at the New York City College

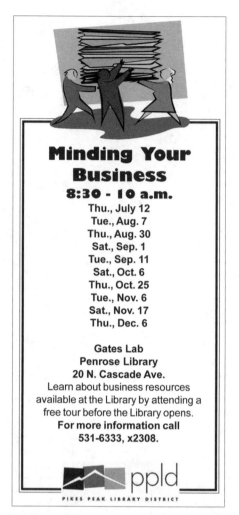

FIGURE 3.2   A resource education program for those starting a business or writing a business plan makes an ideal first program for any new business center.

of Technology to present the program How to Get Started in the Beauty Business. This program covered the ins and outs of starting and running a hair or nail salon. With an array of professionals the program answered many questions, including "What kind of training do I need?" and "What are the rules regarding taxes and tips?" This is a good example of niche programming targeted at a specific need in the area.

Businesspeople are always interested in growing their businesses. No matter what the state of the economy is, programs on marketing and gaining new business are worthwhile. Networking programs have always drawn a good crowd at the Miller Business Resource Center. Businesspeople from companies of all sizes can benefit from networks and networking. A program on the basics of networking is a good place to start:

> How to network
> What is your elevator speech?
> Networking follow-up

The Riverside Public Library hosts a successful program entitled Networking: Schmooze or Lose, Drop the Sales Pitch and Gain New Business. This program is led by a professional publicist and covers effective networking techniques. Again, always consider your business partners when planning a program. Often, they have the expertise you need to have a great program.

After you've shown your patrons how to network, consider offering them actual networking opportunities through programming. As we mentioned earlier in this chapter, the Miller Business Resource Center has a networking component in most programs, but we also offer programs dedicated to networking.

Most businesspeople will participate in a trade show at some point in their careers. (Perhaps a trade show you hold in your library!) Whether they exhibit or just attend, it is important for them to know how to best use their time and experiences:

> Trade show essentials
> How to use trade shows as a networking tool
> Trade show follow-up

These programs are important for the Miller Business Resource Center because we host trade shows at the library. Offering trade show programs helps increase the interest and success of our own trade shows.

Trade shows do not have to be elaborate, multi-day events. Your library can host a trade show for a few hours with some tables and table covers. The Miller Business Resource Center hosts two events each year. These trade shows did not start out big, but success has caused them to grow.

The Women's EXPO (www.womensEXPOli.org), in partnership with the Long Island Fund for Women and Girls, began out of the shared vision of promoting economic independence for women. The goal of the EXPO is to provide a venue for women entrepreneurs on Long Island to market their products, serving as a vehicle to promote economic development as well as networking among women entrepreneurs and women in the business and not-for-profit world. By partnering with over twenty organizations and businesses we are able to put on a successful, well-attended event. Now in its eleventh year, the EXPO has gathered quite a following. We have grown from 20 exhibitors to more than 75 exhibitors, and attendance has skyrocketed to over 2,000. This event takes a lot of work and requires a lot of help from partners. When considering the scope and size of your event, keep staffing issues in the front of your mind. Staff and volunteers from partnering organizations are crucial to your success.

In 2008 the Miller Business Resource Center presented the first annual Strictly Business Tradeshow in partnership with the Brookhaven Chambers of Commerce Coalition and the Greater Middle Country Chamber of Commerce, two organizations that share the vision of promoting economic development on Long Island. The goal of the trade show is to network, promote, and build businesses in the town of Brookhaven. More than 60 companies exhibited and over 400 people attended the show. Now in its fourth year, the event boasts more than 70 exhibitors and over 500 attendees.

Offering incentives and contests can also help bring entrepreneurs to your library. Grant money can enable you to offer monetary incentives. The Brooklyn Public Library has been offering its successful PowerUp! Business Plan Competition for many years. This competition is sponsored by the Citi Foundation and awards monetary prizes for winning business plans. In 2009 the Miller Business Resource Center received a grant from the Citi Foundation to start the same program on Long Island. The Plan! Write! Succeed! Business Plan Competition was created because we know it is crucial that all businesses, no matter how small, have a well thought out and well-defined business plan. Any library can offer a program like this even without prize money. The training, research assistance, and thrill of winning will be enough for some entrepreneurs.

We know that for many, particularly those who are economically vulnerable, self-employment and entrepreneurial ventures can be a viable means of improving their economic condition. Yet, according to the Small Business Administration's Office of Advocacy, new businesses have only a 50/50 chance of surviving for five years or more. While 66 percent of all small businesses survive at least two years, only 44 percent survive for four years. Among the key reasons for business failure are shortcomings in their business planning. A business plan can not only help keep businesses on course, but it is essential for those seeking funding.

Our Plan! Write! Succeed! Business Plan Competition was limited to early-stage ventures, microenterprises, and entrepreneurs who are either in the concept or start-up phase of their business. These are the people that need the most help. Participants were required to attend an orientation session, submit an application to confirm eligibility, and attend four workshops covering the basics of writing a business plan. Over 100 people attended the orientation sessions, with just over 80 submitting applications. Of these people, 57 attended the workshops and only 29 attended all four workshops and were eligible to submit an application.

The training offered through the Plan! Write! Succeed! competition gave these micro-entrepreneurs the skills and edge they need to succeed and flourish. While the competition is the mechanism to attract interest and create the excitement and incentive to complete a business plan, it is the training that is the most important element of this project, with the ultimate goal of producing better-prepared and more viable micro-entrepreneurs for our region. The creation of a business plan is the critical first step in a successful planning process—the blueprint that will guide development and decision making for growing businesses.

The workshops were taught by business counselors from our two local Small Business Development Centers, and the librarians at the Miller Business Resource Center offered business research assistance. Participants not only benefited from the training provided specifically through the competition process; all participants were invited and encouraged to utilize the library's resources. Ongoing networking, training, education, and research opportunities available through the Miller Business Resource Center continue to assist their efforts as the participants move from the planning to the implementation stage of growing their business—connecting them with everything from computer skills training to networking and trade show opportunities to resources for capital investments in their business. Research assistance and access to business counseling continue to be available to assist participants.

Plan! Write! Succeed! was widely publicized throughout Long Island by utilizing the many existing networks and partnerships the Miller Business Resource Center already had in place. A basic flyer and poster was created and distributed via Citibank branches, public libraries in Nassau and Suffolk counties, and other library partners. These partners also helped promote awareness of the competition. By utilizing our partners and local libraries we were able to keep costs down.

The feedback we received for this competition was overwhelmingly positive. Participants loved the workshops and felt they helped them bring their business plans to the next level. Many said that even though they weren't able to submit a business plan, the training and research assistance they received guarantee that they will be able to produce a successful business plan. One of the finalists made this comment: "The classroom environment was a great boost! I thought it was a great experience and with the guidance the classes offered to me, my business plan is in great shape and now available to me for implementation and fine-tuning. Regardless of the outcome I believe it is a win/win for all that participated."

The Burlington County Public Library (BCPL), located in southern New Jersey, consists of a main library in Westampton and seven branch locations. In 2002 the BCPL's administrators realized there was a need for the development of business services in their county, and they recruited the business librarian, Joan C. Divor, to enhance their business reference and to reach out to the Burlington business community. The BCPL saw the potential to strengthen the library's role in the community by enhancing its relationship with this important local customer base.

Divor attended various meetings and events sponsored by the Chamber of Commerce, local business associations, and Small Business Development Centers in order to develop a potential business patron distribution list. She developed the "Business Owner's Toolkit" workshop to create an awareness of all the business information and services available at the BCPL. The workshop was given in two-hour intervals, and the presentation could be viewed on the BCPL's Business Gateway at http://explore.bcls.lib.nj.us/business. Its main objective was to market the library's convenient 24/7 online toolkit and "to build your business know-how."

The BCPL's business center provides one-on-one information meetings with business owners, which have proved to be successful in terms of customer satisfaction and value delivered to the business patron. Divor believes that these meetings have been instrumental in building strong ties with local business owners. The BCPL's Business Gateway features testimonials from the one-on-one meetings, providing concrete examples of how a public library can be an invaluable resource to its business community.

In 2008 the BCPL launched a teen entrepreneurship program, "Make It Pay in a Globalocal Way," for local high students that consisted of a business idea challenge. The BCPL partnered with the Small Business Development Center at Rutgers University and the Friends of the Burlington County Library. The Small Business Development Center assisted by providing judges for the competition, and the Friends donated over $1,500 in cash prizes for the finalists. The program was successful, with 72 student teams entering the competition, leading to 10 finalist teams from which 2 winning teams were awarded cash prizes. The development of the teen entrepreneurship program has strengthened the BCPL's relationship with neighboring schools, especially with the teachers focusing on business curricula. The hope for the future is to expand the library's business-related programs for teens in the area of job readiness and financial literacy.

Divor has found the most successful marketing tool for business programs to be the BCPL calendar and listings in the Small Business Development Center's catalog via their partnership. Speaking at local business meetings and attending networking events have also been effective. Divor has developed an e-mail newsletter, "Biz Currents," which has been an effective communication tool with existing business patrons of the library.

A further example of a successful business program is at the Simsbury Public Library in Simsbury, Connecticut. Started eleven years ago, the Jewel and John Gutman Business Resource Center has grown from 250 to 1,200 square feet and from answering less than 400 business questions in 1999 to 4,000 in 2009. Managed by the business librarian, Jennifer Keohane, a strong advocate for outreach to the business community, workshops have expanded from a handful of sessions to a total of 100 programs.

The popular Wednesday Night Is Business Night workshops that were first attended by about 8–10 people now draw 40–100 attendees. Wired Internet access has given way to wireless, and teaching computer software programs via lecture has been replaced by hands-on technology computer classes in a new twenty-seat Technology Learning Center.

Recent programs include:

> Doing Business with LinkedIn, Facebook and Twitter
> Branding Yourself
> Business Writing: Tools and Inspirations from Master Writers
> Microsoft Excel for Business
> Innovate or Die: Confronting Business Owners
> You've Got to Promote It to Grow It—Grow Your Business with
>   Creative Promotion
> Under Construction: Building Your Resume for College

Keohane, who has a background in marketing and international business, is available for confidential consultations on starting a new business, expanding a marketing plan, solving a business problem, and so on. Keohane also conducts drop-in workshops on Facebook for Business.

Not all of your business patrons are business owners. Some business patrons will look for career guidance from the library's business center. The Miller Business Resource Center offers career counseling to patrons. Counseling is done by professional counselors, and the one-on-one sessions cover everything from job search to resume writing to job transitions. Career programming can be invaluable to business patrons. Programs can target certain audiences such as high school graduates, women returning to work, or workers over fifty (figures 3.3 and 3.4). Programs should be specific to the needs of job seekers. Some popular programs are:

> Transitioning to a new career
> Job search
> Interviewing skills

Miller Center Career Programs

Finding a Job in Today's Economy
Monday, April 20 - 6:30-8:00pm OR Thursday, April 23 - 10:00-11:30am
The current job market is tough to crack. This workshop will provide tips and strategies to find a job in today's challenging economy.

Job Club
Thursdays, April 16 & 30 and May 14 - 10:00-11:00am
Get together with other job searchers to trade information and share sources!

Resumes for Recent College Graduates
Monday, June 8 - 6:30-8:00pm
Are you a recent college graduate? This workshop will focus on crafting a professional resume that will lead you to interviews.

Workplace Success
Monday, May 4 - 6:30-8:00pm
This program covers what you need to know to survive and succeed in the workplace. Topics covered include: dressing for work, getting along with other employees, the dos and don'ts of office politics and managing your time effectively.

Job Opportunities at Stony Brook University*
Thursday, April 9 - 7:00-8:00pm
Representatives from Stony Brook University's Human Resources Services unit will be giving an overview of the recruitment process, giving you all the tips and tricks you need to land a job at Stony Brook. Included in the presentation will be an overview of Stony Brook, how to navigate the Campus Job Opportunities website, and how to make sure your resume gets seen.

* Open to the Public

All classes held at MCPL-Centereach

Please let us know in advance if you require any special accommodations due to a disability
Advance registration is required

MILLER
BUSINESS RESOURCE CENTER
101 Eastwood Blvd., Centereach, New York 11720
575 Middle Country Rd. Selden, New York 11784
631-585-9393
www.mcpl.lib.ny.us

FIGURE 3.3 Smaller career programs targeted to specific audiences are often successful.

Career and College Counseling

When considering a career or college one should see possibilities, not limits. Finding these possibilities is part of what the Middle Country Public Library offers in their Miller Business Resource Center's Career Counseling Center. The Center can provide assistance to unemployed adults and adults re-entering the job market or retraining for a new career, as well as teens approaching college or entering the workforce.

Services include:

- Individual and confidential appointments with a career counselor for employment, occupational, and college counseling
  - Resume preparation assistance
  - College search assistance
- Administration of occupational aptitude and skills assessment tests
  - Financial aid and scholarship information
  - And much more!

Make an appointment today!

Counseling is available to Middle Country Public Library cardholders only.
Please call for an appointment—585-9393 x133.

Please let us know in advance if you require any special accommodations due to a disability.
Miller Business Resource Center
Middle Country Public Library
101 Eastwood Blvd
Centereach, NY 11720
631-585-9393 x133

FIGURE 3.4 In promotional flyers, be sure to indentify specific groups who will benefit from the library's business services.

We have only listed a few successful business programs, but the possibilities are endless. By talking to the businesses in the local area, librarians can determine what would be best for their business patrons.

Everyone's time is important, but for a business person, time is literally money. Be sure that all flyers and press releases describe the program and how it would benefit the business community. If the program speaker is well known in the community, include her name and affiliation on the flyer.

Remember that your programs might not be successful at the start. It may take a lot of experimenting with topics, times, and speakers to get the right mix for your patrons. Keep trying different things and, most importantly, keep talking to your business patrons. You may never have a 100 percent success rate, but you will have business patrons who are happy with your efforts.

4

Marketing
Getting the Word Out

In many ways, marketing a public library business service is no different from positioning a product as unique among many other similar known options. Potential customers for business assistance at a public library usually do not know that such a service exists. Thus, you are promoting a new service to an audience unaware of any benefit or value. Initially, then, the service concept itself has to be introduced to the business community (figure 4.1).

One of the first things we did to establish the business center was to add a separate business reference desk adjacent to the business and career collection. So many times patrons wander amidst the stacks just hoping they will find the information they are searching for. When we inaugurated the business reference desk, we were able to spot people browsing the shelves and offer them assistance. After a while, patrons began to realize we could offer real business help and that was the reason why we were there. Whenever staffing permits, many libraries have instituted a "walking around" librarian who roams the stacks and finds patrons who need help. This not only gives the librarian a chance to find out what people are looking for but also an opportunity to explain other library services.

If you are considering a business service for your library, one way to gauge interest is to advertise the service by signage or flyers in the reference area. An eye-catching flyer outlining the services offered and the materials available could possibly generate attention from business community members. This feedback is important to the center's success.

Adding a separate phone that services the business and career areas facilitates faster service to patrons. We found that business librarians could also keep track of the types of questions asked and what type of information was

Not
Your Ordinary
Business Center

Smart business owners know there is no better way to grow their companies than to become informed. That's what we're all about - Our expert staff will help you find industry facts, consumer trends, and other valuable business information, as well as connect you with prospects and colleagues through our popular networking events.

@

MIDDLE COUNTRY PUBLIC
LIBRARY

www.millerbusinesscenter.org•email:millercenter@mcpl.lib.ny.us•631-585-9393x133

FIGURE 4.1   Begin by introducing the service concept itself to the business community.

needed. Now, librarians and support staff always answer the phone, "This is the Miller Business Resource Center. How may I help you?"

Another possibility is holding a focus group meeting composed of community businesspeople. Demonstrating some of the business resources and discussing their benefits to businesses shows the library's commitment to helping the business community thrive and prosper. For example, for a realtor, showing how you can generate a demographic report of every zip code, or for a prospective dry cleaner, a scatter map of the competition, are real proofs of business data availability.

All employment and motivational literature emphasizes the importance of a good first impression. This is equally true for librarians seeking acceptance in the business environment. Whether at a Chamber of Commerce meeting, a trade show, a workshop, or behind the reference desk, librarians who wear "business dress" are more easily accepted in the business community. Many times we hear, "But you don't look like a librarian!" (Often, these people have not been in a library in many years.) However, to be taken seriously, you have to "dress the part," carry and distribute business cards, and understand the business culture.

When our building was expanded, the business, law, and career collections officially became the Miller Business Resource Center and were headquartered in our new 5,000-square-foot area. All visitors to the library pass a welcome desk, and if they ask for business help or refer to the Miller Business Resource Center, they are directed to the library mezzanine level. As the Miller reference desk is located front and center at the Miller Business Resource Center entrance, librarians are immediately aware of a patron's presence. Also, many phone requests for business reference can be answered by e-mail or fax directly from the business reference desk.

Other features designed to promote the collection and market its services include wall-mounted, multidivisional Lucite holders; these contain multiple copies of flyers that advertise future seminars and workshops for small business and careers and also publicize our services such as resume preparation assistance, career and college counseling, and proctoring. Future programs or series are often promoted with "save the date" flyers listing all upcoming dates, sometimes giving dates over the course of an entire year. It is surprising how many people pick these up and ask for more information or to be signed up. Posters on easels also announce workshops such as the Entrepreneurs

Computer Toolkit (figure 4.2). Recently the Friends of the Library donated a 52" flat-screen television set to the Miller Business Resource Center. Now mounted on a swing arm on the wall near the periodicals, it runs CNBC (on mute) throughout the day, as well as publicizing upcoming programs. The swing arm allows us to move the screen and utilize it for programs we hold in the center.

An additional practice that works well for us is the "round robin." At Library Business Connection and Chamber of Commerce meetings as well as Miller Business Resource Center programs, each attendee stands and gives a one-minute "elevator speech" identifying themselves and relating what they are doing. If possible, at least one of our business librarians attends and uses her minute to announce a new resource, a new program, or a new service for the business community.

Mailings are expensive. However, if an upcoming scheduled business program would interest a certain target audience and a mailing list can be generated for just that business segment, the cost becomes considerably less. For example, a program focused on Doing Business with the Government can be marketed to construction companies, electrical contractors, furniture suppliers, IT companies, and data storage services. Using a business directory database, you can locate all the pertinent businesses in any zip code, county, and so on for your marketing.

Sending a mass e-mail is also an excellent marketing tool. Compiling and maintaining an e-mail list can be done very simply using any e-mail software. Both free and for-purchase programs allow the creation of a distribution list. The Miller Business Resource Center's list contains e-mail addresses of Library Business Connection, Chamber of Commerce, and Women's EXPO members. It is important to make certain that addressees are aware they are opting into the list and can be removed upon request at any time. The effectiveness of the list was apparent at a recent seminar featuring the author of a recent book on self-marketing. In advance of the program, e-mails were sent announcing the program and sign-up procedure. Over forty registrations were received. The audience was a packed house, and only one of the e-mail reserves did not attend.

Our most striking promotional material to date has been our glossy tricolor brochure describing our workplace literacy initiatives, special resources, career counseling and employment information, and education

Entrepreneur's Computer Toolkit

Google Advertising for Entrepreneurs (New!)
Saturdays, May 2, 9, 16 - 9:30am - 11:30am Selden
Learn key words that may attract people to your business website.

Introduction to Power Point for Entrepreneurs
Friday, May 1 - 8:00am - 9:30am Centereach
This introduction to Power Point will help you create professional looking
presentations for your small business.

Introduction to Web Design for Entrepreneurs
Thursdays, May 7, 14, 21 - 7:00pm - 8:00pm Centereach
Learn the basics of web design to build your business presence on the web.

Introduction to Quick Books
Mondays & Tuesdays, June 22, 23, 29, 30 - 6:00pm - 9:00pm Centereach
This course will introduce entrepreneurs to the basic features in QuickBooks and
provide an opportunity for hands-on practice.

MS Office Shortcuts (New!)
Saturday, June 13 - 2:00pm - 4:00pm Selden
This class will help you learn shortcuts for MS Word and Excel as well as Windows.

Search Engine Optimization
Monday, April 13 - 7:00pm - 8:00pm Centereach
This workshop will cover the basic factors that determine what pages rank at the top
of organic search results as well as the issues involved in the pay-per-click advertising
of search engine marketing.

This workshop sponsored by: JPMorganChase

Please let us know in advance if you require any special accommodations due to a disability.
Advance registration is required.
Open to the Public

MILLER
BUSINESS RESOURCE CENTER
@ MIDDLE COUNTRY PUBLIC LIBRARY
101 Eastwood Blvd., Centereach, New York 11720
575 Middle Country Rd. Selden, New York 11784
631-585-9393
www.mcpl.lib.ny.us

FIGURE 4.2   Promote future programs or workshop series with "save the date" flyers listing all
upcoming dates.

and networking opportunities, as well as our business research and online resources. While the business librarians wrote the copy, the printing and graphics design, including a new logo and website, was contracted out to a media relations and graphic design communication company. Librarians met with the designers to review design specifics and approve the layout. While the expense and time required seemed sizable, the result was rewarding. We have a professional brochure that explains, in a nutshell, the goals and offerings of the Miller Business Resource Center. We always have copies at the Miller reference desk and take them to all seminars and workshops. We have had people come to the Miller Business Resource Center, brochure in hand, remarking that they were intrigued by the comprehensiveness of the presentation. The same public relations firm has also assisted us with media publicity. We have found that good media relations people have the right connections and expertise to promote your service or product (figure 4.3).

Since its opening, the Miller Business Resource Center has always been aware of the "power of the press." We have learned that every grant awarded is not only valuable for the funds received but also for the publicity engendered. For example, if a local bank gives funds for a project, the bank manager, the library director, and the Miller Business Resource Center coordinator are sure to be featured with a picture and explanation in the local newspaper. Most organizational and commercial donors expect their grant funds to result in publicity. Their good works create a favorable impression for them and they are perceived as giving back to the neighborhood. And the library is recognized as a vital, deserving community asset.

At first, for us, coverage was limited to a bi-county business newspaper, the Long Island newspaper *Newsday,* and a few small newspapers. However, thanks to the efforts of our dynamic library director and local businesspeople, a local weekly newspaper chain decided to publish an edition especially for our area called *The Times of Middle Country.* We are now featured quite often. As part of the Chamber of Commerce, the Miller Business Resource Center has a weekly small ad on the Chamber page. Once every twelve weeks, we receive a larger column (figure 4.4). We also receive extensive coverage for major events such as our Women's EXPO and Strictly Business Tradeshow.

Even if you cannot afford any paid advertising, most local newspapers will carry nonprofit event listings for free, and many will allow free posting in their electronic versions.

About Us

At the Miller Business Resource Center, we understand that the key to successful business management, sustained growth, and healthy profit margins is speedy access to the best resources in your field. Tools to help your business flourish are right at your fingertips. Expert staff provides access to industry data, consumer trends and other essential business information relative to your specific needs and interests. A variety of networking events and training activities are offered to help you connect with colleagues and prospects. We invite you to visit and learn about what the Center can do for you.

Miller
Business Resource Center

The Center serves as a regional resource and an information hub aimed at businesses, independent entrepreneurs, not-for-profit organizations and individuals. Created to support regional economic development, it responds to the information needs of the business community, promotes a literate and job-ready workforce, and provides employment and career exploration opportunities. Situated within the Middle Country Public Library, the Center is supported by the efforts of the Library, the MCL Foundation, corporations, and government funders. Many services are offered in collaboration with local and regional partners. The Center is named for John D. Miller, a Long Island philanthropist who knows from personal experience the importance of business research assistance to help small businesses and entrepreneurs develop and thrive.

This project is funded by a grant from the U.S. Small Business Administration (SBA). SBA's funding should not be construed as an endorsement of any products, opinions, or services. All SBA-funded projects are extended to the public on a nondiscriminatory basis.

Miller
Business Resource Center

Miller Business Resource Center
Middle Country Public Library
101 Eastwood Blvd., Centereach, NY 11720
www.millerbusinesscenter.org
Email: millercenter@mcpl.lib.ny.us
Phone: 631.585.9393 x133
Fax: 631.585.3670

Miller
Business Resource Center

Meeting the needs of the business community

Education & Networking Opportunities

WORKSHOPS AND SEMINARS
Workshops and seminars that focus on a wide range of topics are essential to the successful entrepreneur. Explore the array of possibilities provided by the Center. Topics include: *Introduction to Business Resources, Marketing Strategies to Grow Your Business, Import and Export Trade Leads, Entrepreneur's Computer Toolkit,* and *Social Networking Tools for the Entrepreneur.*

LIBRARY BUSINESS CONNECTION
The *Library Business Connection* is an education and networking morning meeting for local businesspeople to share resources, exchange information, and participate in educational presentations. Learn about customer service strategies, time management techniques, marketing, finance, investment programs, e-commerce, employment regulations, legal issues, and communication skills.

STRICTLY BUSINESS TRADE SHOW
The *Strictly Business Trade Show* is an annual spring trade show that has been created to promote economic development in the Town of Brookhaven and is geared to businesses involved in retail, service industries, and professional business groups. The *Strictly Business Trade Show* is a cooperative venture with the Greater Middle Country Chamber of Commerce and the Brookhaven Chambers of Commerce Coalition.

WOMEN'S EXPO
The *Women's EXPO,* an annual fall showcase for Long Island women artists and entrepreneurs, serves as a dynamic vehicle to promote economic development and networking among women entrepreneurs and women in the business, arts and not-for-profit world. The *EXPO* is organized and supported through the efforts of many local and regional volunteers, individuals, businesses, and corporate representatives.

"Over the past several years, the Miller Business Resource Center has been a huge asset in both obtaining and sorting information on businesses in the Long Island area. The Center's research librarians provide lists sorted by the company's business operation, geographical location, sales volume, number of employees, or any other category of interest. These lists include essential information on each company, which enables me to work smarter and use my time more efficiently."

- Commercial Real Estate Broker
  Sutton and Edwards

Business Research & Online Resources

The Miller Business Resource Center and BIZLINK, the Center's electronic portal, offer extensive business information. Experienced business librarians provide one-on-one research assistance and connect users with the best resources in their field. The Center helps businesses:

- Access BIZLINK for specialized business databases and recommended websites
- Gather industry trends and market research
- Explore company profiles and market share reports
- Investigate demographic and statistical profiles
- Search legal and not-for-profit sources
- Study human resource management and practices
- Connect to timely workshop and seminar announcements

"I highly recommend using the services at the Miller Center. The employees are extremely professional and helpful. In the past, they have prepared lists of prospective clients, as well as assisted me with research on specific industries. This has been a great help to me as I try to expand my business contacts."

- Vice President & Business Development Officer
  Empire National Bank

Workplace Literacy

To assure a literate and job-ready workforce, a variety of programs that promote basic skill development are offered:

- Group ESOL instruction & English Conversation Groups
- Computer skills training
- One-on-one literacy instruction offered through our partnership with Literacy Suffolk, Inc.
- Workplace readiness
- Citizenship education

"The Miller Business Resource Center has been an extraordinary resource as we continue to expand our business on Long Island and beyond. The data the Center provides is first rate and the turnaround time is remarkable. I highly recommend it to anybody who is serious about prospecting, building a business, or managing a sales effort."

- Executive Vice President / Head of Business Development
  Ronco Paper

Career Counseling & Employment Information

Specialized career information services include one-on-one counseling, extensive collections focused on careers, higher education, employment and training opportunities, and a variety of programs and job fairs. While the collection and many programs are open to all, the counseling services are limited to library district residents only.

www.millerbusinesscenter.org • Phone: 631.585.9393 x133

FIGURE 4.3 Consider contracting a media relations or graphic design group to create a comprehensive brochure for long-term use.

FIGURE 4.4   Submitting articles or writing a periodic column for your local newspaper creates promotional opportunities for your center.

Twice a year, we gather all the pertinent newspaper articles, make copies, and put them together in a house-generated booklet entitled *The Miller Business Resource Center in the News*. We make multiple copies so we can hand these out at trade shows, local business meetings, and community events. We also have a large binder containing reprints of all Miller Business Resource Center publicity and bring it with us to business events.

Once a year the Miller Business Resource Center librarians participate in the Hauppauge Industrial Association's Annual Trade Show, which takes place at the local community college's sports and exhibition plaza. For our display area, we have had a standing banner and a table cover designed with the Miller logo. Copies of our brochure and laptop computers are brought along to demonstrate our services. Like other vendors, we always have an inexpensive "giveaway." Perhaps our most popular one was a magnetic clip with the Miller Business Resource Center name and logo on it. One of the major purposes of marketing is to keep your business or organization name in front of potential customers. If your giveaway is a practical item, people will use it and remember your name and service. We know many of the HIA members and also a number of the businesspeople touring the show, but there are always people who are surprised to see a public library represented. We always explain what we do and always leave with questions from new attendees.

Our partnership with the HIA has grown over the ten years it has been in operation. At first, we were an unknown entity waiting to be tested. Now we are considered an integral part of their association and a vital "member benefit." Many times before businesses join the organization, they call us to tell us the Miller Business Resource Center service is a major reason they are joining.

The HIA has a number of committees dealing with different industries and business topics. At various times during the year, the Sales, Membership, Business Development, and International Trade committees hold one of their monthly meetings at the library, where business librarians give a presentation highlighting the remote online resources available to businesspeople through the partnership with the Miller Business Resource Center. Each committee member also receives a packet of materials that includes a recap of the presentation and an *In the News* pamphlet. This meeting always generates a number of business reference requests not only from the attendees but also from their company staff members, who received the information from their company executive. Quarterly member orientation meetings are also held at the HIA for Miller Business librarians to introduce the service to the new HIA members. Each attendee receives a flyer (figure 4.5) annotating the business databases, and the attendee also meets one or two of the librarians. Invariably, the next day, new HIA members come to the library for a personal tour and to discuss their business information needs.

Four times a year, the Middle Country Public Library mails the *Middle Country Public Library Quarterly* (www.mcpl.lib.ny.us/pdf/full_catalog.pdf), which is an announcement of upcoming programs, to all area residents. All library departments meet together to coordinate dates and meeting spaces for the programs. The Miller Business Resource Center programs are designed to address the issues confronting small businesses and potential entrepreneurs, job seekers and employers, and college and technical school students. Sample programs have included the following:

Basics of Starting Your Own Business
Business and Technical Schools
Career Exploration and Evaluation
Countdown to College: The College Application Process
Doing Business with the Government
Exploring Health Care Careers
Exploring Volunteer Opportunities
Franchising Basics
How to Break into the Comic Book Industry
How to Exhibit Successfully at a Craft Show
Internet Job Search Strategies
Is Your Business Ready? A Contingency Planning Fair
Job Opportunities at SUNY Stony Brook
Planning for College When You Have a Disability
Resume Writing for High School Graduates
So, You Want to Be a Musician?

The Miller Business Resource Center has also recently purchased twenty laptop computers to allow us to offer computer classes for entrepreneurs. With grant funds provided by the J.P. Morgan Chase Foundation, we have

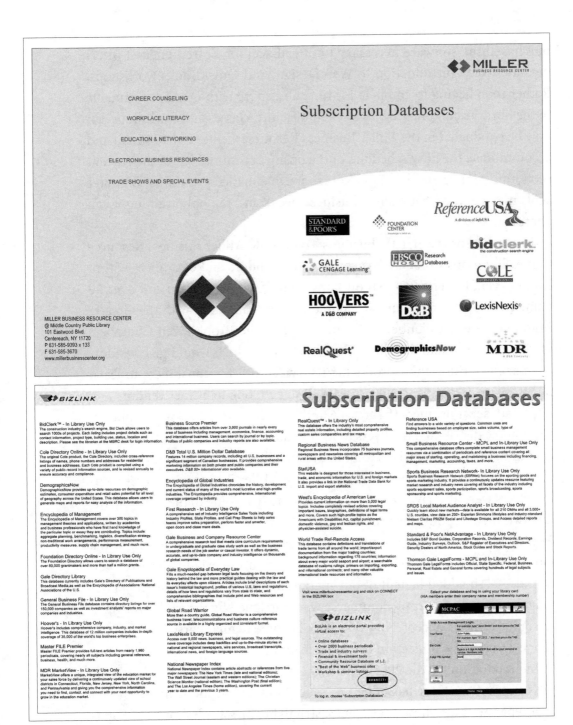

FIGURE 4.5 Distribute annotated lists of your business-related databases to local business or industry groups.

purchased the software necessary to offer Excel for Entrepreneurs, Intermediate Excel, Introduction to Web Design, and QuickBooks workshops. Rather than having to compete for time and space with other departments in the library's computer lab in a satellite facility, classes and workshops can now be conducted in the Miller Business Resource Center environment and accommodate the busy schedules of the business community. In the current economic climate, free business workshops to enhance workforce computer skills may be just what a small business needs and the only training it can afford.

To market for the Strictly Business Tradeshow, Miller Business Resource Center librarians needed to reach potential vendors and customers within Brookhaven, the largest town on Long Island, with 8 villages and over 50 hamlets. The Miller Business Resource Center teamed up with the Greater Middle Country Chamber of Commerce and the Brookhaven Chambers of Commerce Coalition to host the trade show, which would give vendors a chance to exhibit their products or services and for consumers to learn about them. Two different flyers were designed: one to attract vendors and one to attract consumers (figures 4.6 and 4.7). The Brookhaven Chamber of Commerce distributed the flyers to its members—the other chambers in the coalition. Business librarians went to the meetings of five separate chambers to describe the trade show and the role of the Miller Business Resource Center. Flyers were also given to local businesses to distribute to their customers. The two media sponsors of the event, *The Times of Middle Country* and *The Pennysaver,* ran free ads promoting the event. In return, they were given a table at the fair. Over 70 vendors participated in the event, with over 400 attendees. An added benefit of our marketing efforts was that members of neighboring Chambers of Commerce were intrigued by the Miller Business Resource Center concept. Now they have become regular participants in our Library Business Connection breakfast meetings.

In preparation for the 2009 Strictly Business Tradeshow, the Miller Business Resource Center has added a "save the date" announcement linked to a separate trade show page—www.strictlybusinesstradeshow.org. Highlighted are:

an "about" link with time and place, event goal, organizations
    involved, and logos of the major sponsors

The Greater Middle Country Chamber of Commerce • Brookhaven Chambers of Commerce Coalition
Miller Business Resource Center @ Middle Country Public Library

FOR CONSUMERS:

- Meet your community businesses
- Discover local products and services
- Experience *Main Street* @ the Library

FOR BUSINESSES:

- Promote your business
- Network with other community businesses and organizations
- Market your product or service to a wide range of consumers

PROMOTIONAL GIVEAWAYS • LIGHT REFRESHMENTS • DOOR PRIZES

ENTERPRISE SPONSORS

The Verdi Fullenbaum Group
Merrill Lynch

SUFFOLK
Federal Credit Union

VENTURE SPONSORS

BANK of SMITHTOWN
Dedicated. To You.

Commerce Bank
America's Most Convenient Bank®

PARTNER SPONSORS

Allstate/Jeff Freund Agency, Inc.
Holiday Inn Express - Stony Brook
Community Development Corporation of LI
RE/MAX / Jane Zilpelwar
Therese Marcel's Inc.
T.W. English Inc.
Blue Willow Office Environments
WAMU

Times Beacon Record Newspapers

FOR MORE INFORMATION, VISIT OUR WEBSITE AT
WWW.STRICTLYBUSINESSTRADESHOW.ORG
OR CALL 585-9393 EXT. 219

ALL ISLAND Media inc.
PUBLISHERS OF
SHOP LOCALLY
TOWN CRIER PENNYSAVER

FIGURE 4.6 Hosting a tradeshow promotes local businesses and your business center simultaneously.

FIGURE 4.7 Use a modified version of your tradeshow flyer to attract vendors.

    a schedule of events

    vendor applications

    vendor directory

    sponsor opportunity flyer

While the Strictly Business Tradeshow required the participation of Chambers of Commerce and area businesses, the Women's EXPO, now in planning for the eleventh annual event, markets to a different audience. As detailed in chapter 3, the Women's EXPO highlights products made and sold by women. Publicity for this event, held every October, requires the coordination of six committees and media cooperation involving press, TV, and Internet marketing. In addition, flyers are placed by committee members, staff, and volunteers in local beauty parlors, nail salons, boutiques, flower shops, craft outlets, and so on. Both vendors and attendees applaud the event, and attendance has grown from 500 in 2000 to over 2,000 shoppers in 2010. It is an amazing sight to see 2,000 people in a public library! Many attendees are prospective small business entrepreneurs. They have a craft or product and they need assistance with business plans, financing, and marketing. What a unique opportunity this represents for Miller Business Resource Center librarians to explain our partnerships, networking opportunities, and services for new businesses!

For marketing today, a website is essential. For libraries with business services, a website is a powerful tool to provide access to vital subscription databases and key business websites. Also, your website offers a relatively inexpensive way to market upcoming workshops and seminars, future networking events, and connections to partnering organizations. Many library websites now offer online program registration and downloadable event applications.

A coordinated calendar of all local business events can also be a great time-saver for those searching for and also scheduling programs. The Charleston County Public Library (CCPL) Business Center website provides access to a coordinated calendar of business programs in the Charleston area. The CCPL is a member of the Small Business Charleston Resource Network, a collaboration of over twenty organizations and agencies that provide assistance to entrepreneurs and existing small business owners. The event calendar at www.smallbusinesscharleston.org presents a calendar for each month with meeting dates, as well as a general listing with links to all area network events.

Interested prospective entrepreneurs and existing business owners need only access one site to locate available programs, courses, workshops, and so on, and sponsoring organizations can prevent scheduling conflicts and duplication by viewing forthcoming events on the master site.

In marketing, never, ever underestimate the power of word-of-mouth advertising. It may take a few years for your business center to gain recognition. However, if you persevere in helping business patrons and reaching out to local entrepreneurs, the word will spread. When we first started our Library Business Connection meetings, at 8 a.m. on snowy winter mornings, there were occasions when we had fewer than ten people in attendance (and three of them were librarians). Thankfully, the word has spread and we now see 40–50 attendees. Also, as the meetings become increasingly popular, we find more business speakers are attracted and volunteer to give presentations.

5

Networking
Meeting and Greeting

Networking is one of the easiest ways to market your business services. Get out from behind the reference desk and meet the business people you can help. For many librarians, the idea of networking is intimidating. Networking often gets a bad rap. If someone approaches, immediately gives a pitch, and tries to push a product or service, he is not networking, he is selling. Networking is building and developing relationships that are mutually beneficial. The benefits of these relationships can include new customers, new jobs, and new partnerships. Too many people think that by networking they will see immediate results; but networking is about making and building connections. In order to network successfully you must be open and willing to meet new people.

Successful networking takes a lot of practice. Start by meeting or reconnecting with people. Listen to them. By listening to them you learn about what they do, what they are interested in, and what they can offer. Once you know this you may be able to make connections for them with other people you know. These connections and referrals usually don't happen right away. You may know someone for years before you have a referral for them. Even if you can't make an immediate connection, be sure to follow up after a meeting and to keep connecting with them.

So how do you start? If you are new to networking, starting a conversation can be uncomfortable. It is easier just to stick with people you know. Remember, to successfully network when attending meetings or programs with a colleague, you must separate and talk with new people. You already know each other; this is the time to make new connections. Your first approach will be the most difficult one, but as you network more and more, it will become easier—almost second nature.

- *Have an introductory line tailored for each event.* It can be something as simple as, "This is my first time here, can you tell me a little about this organization?"

- *Have an elevator speech prepared that will help you get conversations started.* An elevator speech is a short description of who you are and what you do. It is called an elevator speech because you should be able to say it in the time it takes an elevator to go from the first floor to the top floor. Your elevator speech should be under a minute long and say a lot in a few words. Use your elevator speech to grab the listener's attention and show your enthusiasm for your work. Do not introduce yourself with name, title, and company and consider it an elevator speech. Instead, try something like, "I help businesses get free information to help grow their sales." What business person wouldn't be intrigued? Honing the perfect elevator speech will prove to be invaluable to you in your networking endeavors.

- *Become an effective and engaging communicator.* Start by smiling, looking the person in the eye, listening, and offering genuine conversations. Remember that nonverbal communication is a big part of how we communicate. If you approach a person with your arms crossed and look past them, they will not be receptive to connecting with you.

- *Take advantage of a captive audience.* Talk to the people in line with you at the registration table or buffet line. Always make conversation with the people sitting next to you. Start with something as simple as "Hello."

- *Make notes on the business cards you collect.* At some events you may collect several business cards, but how can you remember who's who when you get to the office the next day? It is helpful to make notes on the cards you collect. These notes can be related to the person's job or can include personal information you may have gained about them. These notes will also help with your follow-up.

- *Follow up.* So you've attended a networking event and collected a fistful of business cards. Now what? Don't just collect business cards to be polite. These cards are valuable components of successful networking. These cards will enable you to follow up. If you collect cards and leave them in your pocket, you are wasting a lot of networking time.

Follow-up contact can be made via e-mail, phone, or written note and should be made within 24–48 hours of meeting. The follow-up need not be elaborate. It can be as simple as an e-mail expressing pleasure in the meeting or thanking them for any helpful information. Include any information or materials you may have discussed. Providing follow-up may be enough to differentiate you from others at the event and helps build solid relationships. Be sure not to make it a sales pitch.

Business librarians should attend as many networking events and programs as they are able. These are important to your success and the success of your library. Business librarians can use networking to spread the word about the services offered through their libraries. Meeting businesspeople is a good way of hearing about their needs and concerns. This will allow you to keep your collection up-to-date and relevant to your users. Businesspeople can also become champions of your library services and connect you with new businesses or funders.

Networking with other librarians, at conferences and through professional organizations, will help gather information on new services and resources.

Networking at the Library

Libraries can add networking to almost any program. Advertise a program to begin a half-hour before the actual program start time. That time allows the program attendees to network with each other. Even something as simple as setting up tables and chairs, instead of just chairs, can help people feel more comfortable networking. Librarians in the crowd can facilitate interaction by helping attendees meet each other. This will also help them hone their own networking skills.

Libraries can start their own networking group. With the recent economic downturn, many libraries have started job clubs. These clubs are small groups of people who meet regularly to talk about job searches and careers. The goal is to support the success of all members and to network with others who may be able to help with members' job searches. Take this a step further and start an entrepreneurs' club at the library. This club would give small business owners or potential entrepreneurs a forum to facilitate meeting and the exchange of ideas and contacts.

Over ten years ago, the Miller Business Resource Center started its own networking group. The Library Business Connection (LBC) is a networking group that provides a forum for local businesses to meet, exchange information, share resources, and participate in educational presentations. The program begins at 8 a.m. with a light breakfast and networking among the attendees. After forty-five minutes or so, a speaker discusses a topic relevant to small business owners, such as customer service strategies, time management techniques, or marketing, e-commerce, and communication skills. Networking continues after a brief question-and-answer session. The LBC has been ideal for networking. We often have groups chatting well after the program has ended.

Libraries can hold their own business-to-business networking events. The Miller Business Resource Center holds two trade shows a year that encourage and promote networking. The Strictly Business Tradeshow is held in partnership with the local Chamber of Commerce and the town's coalition of chambers. It was started to allow local businesses to promote themselves and to network with other local businesses. The Women's Expo features women entrepreneurs who are just starting out. The goal of the Expo is to give these women the opportunity to network with local businesswomen and organizations, which can help them as they grow their businesses.

Libraries can host other networking groups such as the local Chamber of Commerce. Librarians can become active in other local business organizations. These organizations may want to hold a meeting at the library. This gives librarians the opportunity to present the resources they offer to a new group of businesspeople.

Online Networking

We would be remiss if we didn't mention the plethora of social networking tools available now. Some of the most popular with businesses and business people are LinkedIn, Twitter, and Facebook. Online networking tools are only as effective as your handling of them. Many users log onto a social networking site and immediately "friend" everyone they know (or think they know) and then do nothing. If you do nothing, then you are not networking.

When choosing contacts on social networking sites, consider who you have met, might meet, or want to meet at a networking event—colleagues, local businesses, government officials, and so on. When you request a connection, be sure to include a personal note stating why you think you should connect. Once the connection has been accepted, follow up with a thank-you.

On all of these social networking sites, it is important to pay attention to your connections, friends, or followers. LinkedIn allows users to get recommendations. If you have a good experience with someone, consider recommending them. Twitter users follow friends and are able to see what friends are posting. If a friend posts good news, you should send congratulations via Twitter. Be sure to use their @twitter name. Mentions can be invaluable to businesspeople. Each mention is another chance for them to connect with someone new. Facebook users can post comments and recommendations to other users' pages. As with the other networking tools, the more mentions and posts, the more chances for new connections.

Starting to network can be daunting, but steady practice will enable you to master it. Don't wait to be at a networking meeting to network. Once you hone your skills you'll find that networking can be done anywhere.

6

The Power of Partnerships

As the earlier chapters mentioned, the development of a business center in a public library is dependent on many fundamental components, such as space, highly trained librarians, and specialized collections and resources, to not only operate but to be competitive in today's evolving business environment. To continue to grow and thrive as a community business center, it is necessary to leave the traditional boundaries of the library and to build relationships with the local business community. Forming relationships takes much time and effort, but it is key to developing strategic partnerships that will allow for future growth.

According to the *Encyclopedia of Small Business* (Gale), a partnership offers the advantage of allowing the owners to draw on the resources and expertise of the copartners. Partnerships can exist on many levels depending on the goals and needs of the partnering organizations. Ideally, the best type of partnership exists when both organizations share an element of individual participation and there is a true matching of one's resources with the other's needs. Potential partners need to have an understanding of each other's organizational culture and mission before entering into the partnership. A trusting relationship based on mutual respect is also essential. Recognizing the value of the strengths and resources that the other has to offer will foster the relationship. Often the most beneficial partnerships are those that are formed locally in that they bring together individuals that share a common goal of striving to make a difference in their own community. After all, a partnership must bring benefits to both partners.

In the past, public libraries have developed many successful partnerships with community organizations. Partnerships with the business community, however, are less frequent. Library leaders need to be committed to the development of partnerships and communicate their importance to the library staff. Often, the business community is unaware of the resources and services available to them through the public library. This community doesn't fully realize the potential of partnering with a library. Attending meetings and events sponsored by Chambers of Commerce, business organizations, and local economic development agencies is crucial in identifying new business professionals, entrepreneurs, small business owners, and community business leaders.

The Miller Business Resource Center has been fortunate to have many successful partnerships that not only have enriched the center's resources and services but also have enriched those of the partnering organizations and agencies. Various partnerships are highlighted in this chapter to demonstrate the scope and range that a public library can have in its partnerships with the private and public sector.

The LBC/HIA Partnership

Prior to the development of the Miller Business Resource Center, the business collection and services of the Middle Country Public Library operated under the auspices of the Center for Business and Careers (CBC). The Library Business Connection, created in 1995, was a networking group designed to promote local economic development by acting as an educational forum and by linking local business owners and professionals to the resources and expertise of the library (figures 6.1 and 6.2). Business librarians planned five breakfast workshops per year on topics relevant to small business owners, introduced new business resources, and created book displays around the topic to its members. The LBC provided a unique opportunity for local businesses to meet and work with other businesses. On the other hand, the CBC was able to showcase its business resources and services, as well as determine the needs of the business community that were not being met. This allowed the Middle Country Public Library to develop a specialized service that was responsive to the needs of the business community. Although a local bank sponsored the LBC, the CBC had not formed an official partnership with one individual business or community organization that comprised the membership. It did,

➤ Join the LBC...

...and network at regularly scheduled breakfast meetings, utilize personalized reference service and receive special mailings. Each breakfast meeting is organized to include speakers on subjects of interest to the members. Special library resources are introduced at each meeting and various materials are available to peruse and/or borrow.

All business and professional members of the community are invited to join the network. Partners are entitled to a courtesy card at the participating libraries. Courtesy cards are provided on an individual basis for one year with special permission.

For further information on how to become an LBC partner, consult the Adult Reference Department at either Middle Country Public Library, 585-9393 or Sachem Public Library, 588-5024.

➤ Access Business Resources

Management	Industry Reviews and
Marketing	Investment Services
Small Business Legal	Resumes
and Tax Information	Cover Letters
Career Development	Interviewing Skills
Sales	Job Search Techniques
Motivation	and more
Customer Service	

Join the LBC for personalized reference assistance.

LBC Library Business Connection

Strengthening Economic Development in Our Community

The Power of Partnership

?

With the combined resources of your "Partners," you'll find:

Have Questions?

Need Answers?

- education & training programs
- employment options
- local laws and ordinances
- time management techniques
- the law and local business
- employment regulations
- customer service strategies
- networking opportunities
- communication skills
- and much, much more!

➤ Our Mission

The Library Business Connection is a network designed to promote local economic development and employment opportunities, and to assist individuals and organizations to access existing resources.

The partnership encourages communication and cooperation among local businesses, government agencies, and educational institutions, including libraries, and cultural organizations and act to strengthen networks, maximize resources, and support individual and organizational development in our region.

With input from its business partners, participating libraries provide a clearinghouse of business resources as well as special reference, program, and bibliographic services.

➤ Our History

In October 1995 the administration and several adult reference service librarians from the Middle Country Public Library met with business and professional members of the community to explore the library's potential for supporting economic development activities in the community.

The library contracted with a consultant who conducted business focus groups in which participants from the business community expressed their interest in a partnership with the library. That information, used in conjunction with the library's already defined mission to reach out to the community, formed the framework for the LBC.

Library Business Connection

Steering Committee

Middle Country Public Library
Sachem Public Library
personalized reference service, special resources, courtesy cards

J.S. Services, Accounting

P. Zarkadas P.C.
Attorney-at-Law

European American Bank

Centereach Rotary

Suffolk County Community College
telecourses, technicenter, skills/vocational training, avocational instruction

State University at Stony Brook School of Professional Development
non-credit, new business, small business, employer/employee training, and labor relations

The Museums at Stony Brook
cultural/educational programs, volunteer opportunities "Perfecting the Art of Business" events

Suffolk County Department of Labor

University Hospital and Medical Center at Stony Brook Health Care Teleservices
call center for health, medical, insurance and HMO queries

Chiropractic Family Care Sports & Spinal Rehabilitation

SanDen Consulting Corp.
Human Resources Consulting
special employer/employee training

Seigerman-Mulvey Co., Inc.
Insurance Brokerage

Borders Books and Music

The Little Computer Shop

Metro Specialty Marketing

Listen to your business neighbors:

"Through the LBC, I found out how I can make my business grow."

"....helped me succeed at my home-based business. The Library had the resources I needed for start-up and the Connection helped me meet other home-based businesspeople. The LBC offers guidance and information."

"When I really needed help with my mail order business, I made the right move, I turned to the LBC. Soon I was on the right track, and back in business!"

"When I wanted to expand my warehouse, the LBC introduced me to local zoning and environmental laws. As a partner, I networked with local architects and owners of construction companies. By using local companies, I helped our community and myself."

Who is the LBC for?
- Small Business Owners
- Professional and Private Practitioners
- Entrepreneurs
- Home-Based Business Owners
- Service Providers or Tradesmen
- Manufacturers
- Educational and Cultural Institutions
- Non-profit Organizations and Agencies

Partial support for the LBC is provided by
Fleet Bank

The Library, the Community, and Your Business... a Partnership that works for all of us

Join the Library Business Connection

Middle Country Public Library	**Sachem Public Library**
585-9393	588-5024

FIGURE 6.1   A precursor to the Miller Business Center, the Library Business Connection acted as an educational forum linking local business professionals and the library.

VOLUME VII NUMBER 3
WINTER 1995

News and Information from your Community Library

Library Business Connection Created

Honoring the library's tradition of reaching out to individuals and groups, 29 business people and professionals participated in Focus Groups this fall and the *Middle Country Library Business Connection* was created. The *Connection* is a network of local businesses, community organizations and the library.

Join the *Middle Country Library Business Connection* for special mailings, networking meetings and personalized reference service. Help us develop the library's business services and resources. Become a member by calling the Adult Reference Department at 585-9393 or stop in at the library.

Thanks to the Focus Group participants for their input and enthusiasm.

Linda Altenburger	Registered Dietitian
Bob Baron	Century 21
John J. Belmonte	Middle Country Central School District
Fred Bergmann	Speedy Sign-O-Rama USA
Peggy Bergmann	Speedy Sign-O-Rama USA
Irv Bornstein	Miller Associates Real Estate
Lawrence Buscemi	Buscemi & Buscemi, Attorneys-at-law
Frank Cappuccio	Computers By Design
Gina Fontanella-Selg	European American Bank
Jim Frayne	Attorney-at-law
Laurel Garbarini	Borders Books
Tom Haggerty	National Westminster Bank
Andrew Hoehler	Rave Cleaners
Barbara Hoehler	Rave Cleaners
Evan A. Karpf	Chiropractic Family Care Sports & Spinal Rehabilitation
Charles Kelly	Centereach Rotary
Karen Knight	The Prudential
Richard Metro	Metro Specialty Marketing
Carrie Mitchell	Century 21
Diane O'Callaghan	Creative Signs By Diane
Jim O'Callaghan	Creative Signs By Diane
Derek Peterson	Computers By Design
John Rose	Lighthouse Agency
John Selvaggio	Firestone Tire & Service Centers
Barbara Smith	Little Computer Shop
Robert Sternberg	Long Island Paneling, Ceilings & Floors
John Suriano	J. S. Services, Accounting
Barbara M. Weltsek	Attorney-at-law
Evie Zarkadas	P. Zarkadas, P.C., Attorney-at-law

The *Middle Country Library Business Connection* is a network of local businesses, community organizations and the library.

In This Issue...

Young Children Learn
at the Library   page 3

Library Tours Under Way   page 2

$7500 Grant Awarded   page 2

Travel the Information Highway
page 2

Authors Demonstrate "How to Talk"

Library Director Sandra Feinberg joined authors Elaine Mazlish and Adele Faber at the library's Reception and Book Signing. Faber and Mazlish, known for "How to Talk So Kids Will Listen and Listen So Kids Will Talk" and their newest volume "How to Talk So Kids Can Learn At Home and In School," appeared before a captivated audience describing ways in which adults and children can successfully communicate. The event was hosted by The Suffolk Family Education Clearinghouse and The Friends of the Middle Country Public Library.

FIGURE 6.2   The announcement of the creation of the LBC highlights services as well as listing business leaders involved in its creation.

however, foster collaboration with the entire local business community that would eventually lead to future innovative partnerships.

In 1999 a mutual board member of the Middle Country Library Foundation and the Hauppauge Industrial Association suggested to Sandra Feinberg, the library director, that the two organizations partner in order to share business resources. At the time, the HIA was an 800-member business organization comprised of business professionals and owners working in Suffolk and Nassau counties but predominantly located in the Hauppauge Industrial Park. The HIA was seeking to create a business library for its members, and the Center for Business and Careers was striving to reach the next level of growth by being recognized as a regional business center on Long Island. Both organizations met and agreed it would be mutually beneficial to the members of the HIA and the CBC to form this unique partnership. The members of the HIA would not only have access to a greater pool of business resources, but they would also have access to the expertise of the business librarians. The CBC, on the other hand, would reach beyond its local business community and become more involved regionally. The CBC and the HIA jointly obtained a $50,000 grant through then Senator Jack Lack to make the partnership a reality.

Once the partnership was solidified and the grant funds were obtained, the mutual goals of the partnership were outlined. The first priority was to develop a method by which library resources could be shared with the members of the HIA. The CBC possessed many specialized business databases in its collection, but now it had to provide remote access to the HIA. A website consultant was hired to develop the LBC-HIA website and to create a password-protected log-in page. Links to the website were placed on both the Middle Country Library's and HIA's home pages. Although the website contained information explaining the partnership and included many free business websites organized by category, its main purpose was to provide access to the CBC's electronic resources. Library patrons were required to input their library bar code in order to gain access to the databases, but the challenge was to provide remote access to HIA members. The business librarians discovered that the HIA assigned individual codes to its members when they joined. The CBC decided to enter the following HIA member information into its Innovative circulation system: company name, contact person, address, telephone number, and HIA code. HIA members would be able to use their individual HIA codes in place of a library bar code to access the business database remotely, and their information would be verified against the library's circulation system. In order to stay current with the HIA's membership, the HIA provided the CBC with a monthly list of existing members, new members, renewals, and deletions. Of course, this whole process would also allow the CBC's print and media collections to circulate as well.

While the LBC-HIA website was being developed, the CBC focused on the types of businesses and business professionals that comprised the members of the HIA in order to better understand the organization. The business librarians decided to create a survey that would be distributed to the various committees that the HIA had developed to cater to targeted industries. Instead of mailing the surveys, the librarians attended the committee meetings, explaining the partnership and distributing the surveys. They were not only able to explain the importance of the survey, but they were able to collect the completed surveys (figure 6.3). The survey proved to be an extremely useful collection development tool and a means to gauge the perception of the HIA membership of what a public library would be able to provide. In order to introduce and market the partnership, the HIA distributed a flyer to its entire membership (figure 6.4).

Operating within a public library, the business librarians of the CBC were accustomed to answering business reference questions while they were physically sitting at the reference desk. The creation of the partnership created the need to provide reference service in a nontraditional manner. The majority of the HIA members were not physically coming to the library to ask for information. They were asking for information over the telephone or by e-mail, so the delivery of information was handled by telephone, e-mail, or fax. A business question logbook was instituted in order track the HIA members that were served, the types of questions that were answered, and the number of hours needed to complete the request (figure 6.5). Furthermore, it also served as a statistical record. Today, the librarians log all business questions on a mutually shared Excel file.

The business librarians began to regularly attend meetings of select HIA committees, monthly business luncheons, and the HIA's annual trade show. Depending on committee objectives, they were asked to conduct workshops on topics relative to the committees' interests, develop bibliographies, and

HIA
Hauppauge Industrial Association

NEW!

DO YOU EVER NEED ACCESS TO BUSINESS-RELATED INFORMATION?

HIA MEMBER BENEFIT!

Look no further! Without leaving the comfort of your office, the world of business information is being placed at your fingertips...at no cost...and with minimal effort.

As a result of HIA's recent partnership with Middle Country Public Library's Center for Business and Careers, a collection of more than 7,000 print and electronic business resources, the Community Resource Database of Long Island, and personalized reference services are being made available **only** to HIA members. This partnership has been funded through a member item grant from Senator James Lack with additional support from People's Alliance Federal Credit Union, State Bank of Long Island and Dun and Bradstreet.

What does this mean to you?

For example, if you need to know who your competitors are for a particular product, you can:

1. Call the HIA/Library hotline and request this information from a research librarian

Or...

2.) Use your special HIA password and access a vast array of on-line resources at **no charge** at **http://lbc-hia.org**. Many of these resources would be quite expensive or prohibitive for you to purchase independently.

In order to make this program successful for you, we need to understand your specific needs. Please take a few moments to answer these questions. Your responses will help in the selection of additional resources for the collection.

LBC/HIA Information Needs Survey

1. Would you rate your need for external information (published outside of your organization) as:

   ____ Daily or several times per week
   ____ Weekly or two/three times per month
   ____ When starting new projects or responding to a specific inquiry.

2. In order to perform your work at optimum levels, your need for information on the following subjects is:

Please check one column for each category.	Critical	Important	Moderately Important	Not Necessary
Annual Reports				
General Business News				
Company Profiles				
Industry News & Trends				
Financial Info				
Market Research Data				
Information Technology				
Vendor/Supplier Info				
Industry Patents				
Industry Standards				
Stock Prices				
Technical Journals				

3. What types of information required for your work have been most difficult for you to obtain? Why?

_____

_____

_____ **over**

FIGURE 6.3 Results from the LBC's HIA members served as a collection development tool and gauged the HIA members' perception of what a public library would be able to provide.

4. How do you typically obtain the information you need? Rank 1-8, with 1 being what you would do first:

   ___ Use local Public or Academic library
   ___ Internet
   ___ Internal Databases
   ___ Personal journal subscriptions
   ___ Consult with a colleague
   ___ Hire a consultant
   ___ Contact Professional Society
   ___ Government Agencies
   ___ Other (Please specify_____)

5. Which periodicals from the following list would be helpful to you in your business? Please choose from the following list and/or add additional titles useful to you.

   ☐ Advertising Age   ☐ HR Magazine Inc.
   ☐ Brown's Business Letters   ☐ Industry Week
   ☐ Business Marketing   ☐ L.I. Business News
   ☐ Business Week   ☐ Management Today
   ☐ Chain Store Age   ☐ New York State Contract Reporter
   ☐ Commerce Business Daily   ☐ New York Times
   ☐ Crain's N. Y. Business   ☐ Newsday
   ☐ Forbes   ☐ Sales & Marketing Management
   ☐ Fortune   ☐ Wall Street Journal
   ☐ Franchising World   ☐ Others

6. Do you have Internet access?   7. Would access to a Home Page with Business Information help you?

   ☐ Yes   ☐ No
                                              ☐ Yes   ☐ No

8. How would you like information delivered to you?

   ☐ Electronically   ☐ Print   ☐ Both

9. Please indicate which workshops you would be interested in attending.

   _____ How to use the Internet and World Wide Web in Business.

   _____ How to find information on an industry.

   Which industry? _____

   _____ How to effectively use available Business Databases.

   _____ Other _____.

10. Would telephone access to address your research needs be of help to you? ☐ yes   ☐ no

Please return survey to: **HIA**
                         P.O. Box 11004
                         Hauppauge, NY 11788

   (516) 543-5355
   fax (516) 543-5380

Name _____ **Company** _____
phone# _____ **fax#** _____
e-mail _____

1/00

FIGURE 6.3   (cont.)

★ Business Research Just Got Easier! ★

YOU MAY HAVE RECENTLY READ IN NEWSDAY, SUFFOLK LIFE OR THE DAILY NEWS ABOUT THE NEWLY FORMED PARTNERSHIP BETWEEN HIA AND MIDDLE COUNTRY PUBLIC LIBRARY. THIS VENTURE WILL PROVIDE INCREDIBLE BUSINESS RESEARCH CAPABILITIES TO HIA's 800 MEMBER COMPANIES.

Please call the HIA office for your company's **PRIVATE ACCESS CODE** which will give you entre to a unique service only available to HIA members (631-543-5355).

WHAT'S IN IT FOR YOU?

Business Research assistance will be provided by highly qualified business librarians and faxed directly to your office...

Or...

Do your own research on-line by accessing business databases available through the joint Middle Country Public Library/HIA website.

WHAT WILL IT COST YOU?

$0.

Courtesy of Senator Lack and with the support of People's Alliance Federal Credit Union and State Bank of Long Island, expensive on-line business databases and Middle Country librarian research assistance will cost you absolutely nothing – as long as you maintain your HIA membership and grant money is available.

WHAT INFORMATION IS AVAILABLE ON-LINE AND HOW CAN IT BE ACCESSED?

A partial list of on-line business databases includes:

Associations Unlimited	Info USA
Corp Tech	National Newspaper Index
Hoover's Company Profiles	Health Source Plus
Infobase Telephone Directory–U.S. Business	Brands and Their Companies
& Residential	Business Source-Premier & Elite
Community Resource Database (CRD)	General Business File

...And much more

- Over -

P.O. BOX 11004, HAUPPAUGE, NEW YORK 11788 • (516) 543-5355 • FAX: (516) 543-5380
E-mail: info@hia-li.org • Web Site: http://www.hia-li.org

FIGURE 6.4   In order to introduce and market its partnership with the LBC, the HIA distributed a flyer to its entire membership.

Where can I find the latest information on the best laser fax machines for business?

What is the number of pharmaceutical firms with addresses and contact persons in Omaha, Nebraska?

To reference any of the databases, or for a description of each –
Log on to LBC-HIA.ORG (or you may link to LBC-HIA.ORG
from the HIA Website: HIA-LI.ORG).

HOW CAN A LIBRARIAN BE CONTACTED FOR RESEARCH ASSISTANCE?

Call 585-9393 x 216 or x 219 or e-mail to busref@mcpl.lib.ny.us
(Be sure that you know your company access code.)

WHEN WILL THESE SERVICES BE AVAILABLE?

Immediately.

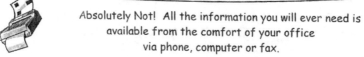

DO YOU NEED TO GO TO THE LIBRARY?

Absolutely Not! All the information you will ever need is
available from the comfort of your office
via phone, computer or fax.

In an ongoing effort to make life easier by providing
pragmatic services and programs to address your business needs,
HIA invites you to make use of this valuable member benefit!

*Watch your mail for announcements of HIA Seminars which will teach you how to
easily navigate these databases and find exactly what you need*

Research At Your
Fingertips!

P.O. BOX 11004, HAUPPAUGE, NEW YORK 11788 · (516) 543-5355 · FAX: (516) 543-5380
E-mail: info@hia-li.org · Web Site: http://www.hia-li.org

FIGURE 6.4 (cont.)

Date: _____ Librarian: _____

Client Information
(Please print clearly)

Name	
Affiliation	
Business	
Address	
E-Mail	
Phone	Fax

Reference Request

Contact Log
(Please initial each contact)

Date	Contact	Reason for Contact

(See next page for additional log)

Comments	
Disposition	

Date Completed: _____

FIGURE 6.5 Keeping a reference question log will aid in future service and act as a statistical record.

serve as panelists. The following are examples of the topics presented at various events:

> Competitive Intelligence
> How to Use Research to Create Sales
> International Business Resources
> Nearby Sources for Far Away Trade
> Resources for the HR Professional
> Roadmap to Resources

Committees have also held their monthly meetings at the Miller Business Resource Center, where the business librarians were able to explain how the partnership works, demonstrate databases, and introduce print resources. Appointments are also made on a regular basis with HIA members who possess in-depth research requests.

The partnership between the Miller Business Resource Center and the Hauppauge Industrial Association has endured for eight years. Throughout that time, Miller Business Resource Center and HIA staffs have changed and grown, policies and procedures have been evaluated and adjusted, and consistent funding has been a challenge, yet the partnership is thriving more than ever. Initially, the librarians were asked, "Why is the library here?" Now they are accepted as one of the members with a valuable service to offer. Recently, the Miller Business Resource Center has been invited to be a member of the HIA Front Line Team, which was developed to provide immediate assistance to businesses at risk. The Miller Business Resource Center staff has spearheaded the compilation of a roster of local, state, and federal agencies providing technical and operating assistance, low-cost financing, and economic incentive and development programs, as well as employee retention and recruitment programs.

The Community Development Corporation of Long Island

The Community Development Corporation (CDC) of Long Island is a non-profit organization devoted to helping Long Islanders achieve self-sufficiency and long-term economic stability by assisting with first-time home-buying, sustaining affordable homeownership, starting or expanding a business, and acquiring personal and business financial management skills. The CDC of Long Island is located right in Centereach, New York, approximately one-quarter mile from the library. The CDC developed a Core Four Business Planning Course for existing small business owners, aspiring entrepreneurs, or anyone with a business idea; the course runs for four sessions, a total of twelve hours. The program provides training in the following areas: success planning, market planning, cash flow planning, and operations planning.

The CDC of Long Island had been a sponsor of the Miller Business Resource Center's Women's Expo and an existing member of the Library Business Connection. Both organizations share the mutual goal of providing economic development to small business owners and entrepreneurs, so it seemed logical that the CDC selected the Miller Business Resource Center to hold its Core Four Business Planning Course for women entrepreneurs. The Miller Business Resource Center is able to provide a training room for the program and assists in marketing it to its business patrons, although the CDC handles registration. A business librarian participates in teaching the "market planning" segment of the program by introducing reference tools to research demographic information, industry profiles, and sample business plans. The Core Four Business Planning Course began meeting at the Miller Business Resource Center in 2002 and continues to meet regularly, hosting twelve workshops annually.

The Small Business Development Center at the State University of New York at Stony Brook

Small Business Development Centers (SBDCs) throughout the country provide free one-on-one counseling to entrepreneurs who want to start a business and to current business owners interested in improving the performance of their existing business. The SBDC at Stony Brook is located seven miles from the Middle Country Public Library, and both organizations share the common mission of fostering the stability and growth of small businesses on Long Island. The business librarians have had a long-standing relationship with the SBDC's counselors and often refer patrons to the SBDC when needed. On a yearly basis, the librarians have provided an overview of the Miller Business Resource Center and the new resources that are available to them. The Miller Business Resource Center and the SBDC have worked in conjunction to offer free programs to the public on the following topics:

Basics of Starting a Home-Based Business
Basics of Starting Your Own Business
Financing Your Own Business
Marketing and Advertising Your Business
Starting a Home-Based Daycare Business

In 2003, after the Middle Country Public Library underwent an extensive renovation, the Miller Business Resource Center had three new meeting rooms available for community partners to use. It was a natural progression of the existing partnership to move to the next level. The library approached the SBDC at Stony Brook, and they agreed to send a business counselor to the Miller Business Resource Center one day per week to offer business counseling. All appointments and inquiries are made through the SBDC's office. On-site, however, counselors have access to private office space, a computer, telephone, and of course, all the resources of the Miller Business Resource Center. Library patrons, who found the university setting intimidating or had transportation problems, were thrilled to be able to meet at the library. The partnership between both organizations has proved to be beneficial in targeting and marketing to the same patron/client base. The library patrons seeking business information and resources are also potential clients for the SBDC and vice versa.

Throughout the years, the Miller Business Resource Center and the SBDC at Stony Brook have continued working together by providing reciprocating referrals, presenting at local business events and seminars, and striving to provide the most accurate and timely information to a shared local business community. In 2009 the partnership was taken to a more collaborative level. The Miller Business Resource Center applied for a grant from the Citi Foundation to host a business plan competition that would educate potential small business owners and entrepreneurs as well as offer the opportunity to win cash prizes for the best business plan. One of the grant stipulations was that the Miller Business Resource Center had to reach out to potential participants in both counties of Long Island, Suffolk and Nassau. The Miller Business Resource Center contacted the two SBDCs located on Long Island, Stony Brook and Farmingdale, to ascertain if they would be interested in working collaboratively to provide the training component of the business plan competition. The SBDCs agreed to partner with the Miller Business Resource Center, the Stony Brook SBDC focusing on the residents of Suffolk County and the Farmingdale SBDC focusing on the residents of Nassau County. The grant was submitted and Citi Foundation awarded the funds to the Miller Business Resource Center to implement the Plan! Write! Succeed! Business Plan Competition. The three organizations held meetings and conference calls to schedule the trainings, implement rules and guidelines, and other pertinent logistics related to the competition.

The Brooklyn Public Library and the Queens Economic Development Center have been past recipients of the Citi Foundation business competition grant. Miller Business Resource Center librarians visited the librarian that first implemented the business competition at the Brooklyn Public Library and asked for suggestions and advice throughout the development of Plan! Write! Succeed!

Greater Middle Country Chamber of Commerce and Brookhaven Chambers of Commerce Coalition

For more than ten years, the Middle Country area did not have its own Chamber of Commerce. In 2005, a local bank branch manager decided it was time to establish the Greater Middle Country Chamber of Commerce, developing a membership of 100 members during the first year. The meetings were held at local area restaurants, but as the membership increased, meeting space became an issue. The Miller Business Resource Center offered the library's community room for the chamber's monthly meetings and allowed the chamber to house files, brochures, and giveaways at the library. The business librarians attend monthly meetings and volunteer on numerous chamber committees. Holding chamber meetings at the library has proved to be an incredible opportunity to network with local business owners and market the services of the Miller Business Resource Center, reaching a segment of the business population that may not have thought to approach the public library. Currently, the Greater Middle Country Chamber of Commerce hosts a new member orientation at the Miller Business Resource Center prior to the monthly meetings. The Miller Business Resource Center is introduced as a member benefit for joining the chamber, and a business librarian is always in attendance to provide a brief overview of the resources and programs available to small businesses.

The mission of the Brookhaven Chambers of Commerce Coalition (BCCC) is to represent all the Chambers of Commerce that are within the boundaries of the town of Brookhaven and to support the vast numbers of businesses and professionals who are members of these chambers in a uniform voice on common issues and concerns. It also seeks to sponsor seminars to help aid small businesses, and that goal is how the Miller Business Resource Center and the BCCC formed a partnership. They approached the Miller Business Resource Center wanting to sponsor an existing program or workshop. The Miller Business Resource Center had always wanted to host a small business trade show that would cater to service-oriented businesses and, with the support of the BCCC, thought that a trade show could be organized. The Greater Middle Country Chamber of Commerce was asked to participate, and the three organizations joined forces to organize the Strictly Business Tradeshow. The purpose of the trade show is "to network, promote, and build businesses in the Town of Brookhaven." A planning committee was formed with members from the partnering organizations, sponsors of the trade show, business support organizations, and community groups. The first Strictly Business Tradeshow was held on May 6, 2008, with over seventy retail and service-oriented industries represented. The goal is to make the Strictly Business Tradeshow an annual event and to expand it to include workshops and presentations. The success of the partnership between the three organizations and ultimately the Strictly Business Tradeshow was the shared vision of promoting economic development on Long Island.

7

Funding
How to Pay for It All

Operating a business center within a public library requires a commitment from the library administration to designate a certain amount of library funding to manage it. How individual libraries allocate funds for the development of new collections and resources will of course vary. Many libraries don't have adequate budgetary funding to meet community needs, let alone develop new library services. Traditionally, public libraries rely on local, state, federal, and private funding to operate. Approximately 80 percent of libraries receive a significant portion of their annual budget from local tax dollars, and this is seen as the most reliable and basic form of funding. The annual budget will cover basic budget lines of funding such as books, subscriptions, programs, and equipment, but it will not provide the monetary support to develop a specialized center or service. Librarians have had to turn to other sources of funding to supplement the basic library budget, including grants from the public and private sector, foundations, Friends of the Library groups, philanthropists, and fund-raising events.

Pursuing grants as an additional funding stream requires a commitment from the library administration to designate staff who will be devoted to the entire grant process, including writing, submitting, and managing the grant from start to finish. The grant application process can be rigorous because each agency, government or private, will have distinct guidelines, deadlines, and methods of submission. Grant writing should begin with the identification of a clearly defined project or program, and the library's mission and goals should be incorporated into the planning process.

There are a variety of resources and workshops available to assist with both the grant search and the grant-writing process. Grant seekers should familiarize themselves with the Foundation Center, a national nonprofit service organization considered to be the nation's authority on organized philanthropy, providing grant seekers with a wide array of research tools and educational programs. The Foundation Center has five regional library/ learning centers and 400 funding information centers located at libraries, not-for-profit centers, and organizations throughout the United States. The Foundation Center's *Foundation Directory Online* is a subscription-based database that includes 95,000 U.S. foundations and corporate donors and approximately 1.3 million grants, searchable by grant makers, companies, grants, and 990s. The Foundation Center's website (www.foundationcenter .org) also offers free searchable information and its print directory, *The Foundation Directory,* includes listings for private and public foundations and corporations. The *Library Grants Blog* (www.librarygrants.blogspot.com) is a free website, developed in 2005, to assist librarians with the grant-seeking process. National and large regional grants are posted on a monthly basis, and grant opportunities are verified to ensure that libraries are eligible to apply.

Browsing library journals and periodicals can also be helpful to find new library grant opportunities, but they also provide information on past giving opportunities and the recipients. *Grants for Libraries Hotline* is a monthly newsletter providing grant opportunities for libraries as well as the educa-tion community. Entries include grant descriptions, eligibility requirements, deadlines, fund amounts, and contact information. On the American Library Association's website there is a listing of awards, grants, and scholarships that can be searched (www.ala.org/ala/awardsgrants/grants/). These are just a few examples of the resources available.

As librarians, we are comfortable with daily library responsibilities such as assisting our patrons, researching questions, selecting resources, catalog-ing materials, and scheduling programs. Often, seeking funding outside of the traditional sources can be intimidating and overwhelming. Becom-ing familiar with general fund-raising resources will also be beneficial to the grant-seeking process. *Advancing Philanthropy,* a bimonthly magazine published by the Association for Fundraising Professionals (AFP), focuses on educating and informing fund-raisers. AFP members receive the publi-cation with their membership, but subscriptions to nonmembers are also available. The AFP website (www.afpnet.org/) hosts a wealth of information, including a Resource Center with a comprehensive "Hot Topics" overview of key fund-raising areas that its members identified as being in demand. The Grassroots Institute for Fundraising Training publishes the *Grassroots*

Fundraising Journal and is geared to small or medium-sized nonprofits. The journal's articles focus on practical strategies and information to assist nonprofit organizations, board member involvement, volunteerism, and marketing strategies.

Relationship building and networking are also an integral part of the grant process, and the time dedicated to the development of these relationships needs to be factored into the time spent on individual grants. The same principles used for forming partnerships can be used to create relationships or make contacts with the private sector. Banks and corporations have separate foundations whose mission is to support key community initiatives. Forming a relationship with a local branch bank manager, business development officer, or community relations representative can lead to future funding. Of course, it could take a few years to form the foundation of these relationships, and from experience, we know that employees move on to other positions or places of employment and new relationships need to be formed again. However, if pursing grants becomes a viable form of funding for a public library, it will be necessary to not only create relationships but maintain them as well.

Partnerships with other organizations are beneficial on many levels, and they can also be beneficial to the grant application process. At times, your library's mission or scope of services alone will not be sufficient to fulfill a grant request. However, in conjunction with another institution, the grant request may be feasible by blending the experiences and relationships of two organizations. One of the organizations will need to take the lead with the grant application process, but the development of the proposal, objectives, and budget should be a joint effort. Planning meetings will be imperative to develop a clear and defined role for each organization.

Grant-making foundations or entities require organizations to submit quarterly, midyear, or final reports as evidence that grant funds were spent as specified in the grant proposal. At the beginning of the grant process, most applications request the following: objectives, needs assessment, goals, program budget, and evaluation methods. Tracking accurate statistics throughout the funding year is imperative to fulfill the reporting requirements, as well as prove to the funder the effectiveness of your organization's program and highlight that all goals and objectives have been met. Detailed statistics should present a clear picture of how funds were utilized and justify the needs assessment. For a first-time grant application, documented statistics will allow a new funder to understand the scope of your program or the mission of your organization. Furthermore, they will demonstrate your organization's effectiveness in the community. If you are resubmitting for another grant, you will have the proper tools to prove your program success and argue your case for future funding.

Setting realistic grant objectives and goals will also make the reporting process more efficient. Creating a list of milestones will allow you to review what has been accomplished in the grant cycle and what still needs to be addressed. Sometimes, due to unforeseen circumstances, not all objectives or goals can be met. It's better to acknowledge that fact during the grant cycle rather than explain to a funder at the final reporting process why these goals or objectives haven't been met. Having an open line of communication with your funder will ease the process, and hopefully, a new direction can be taken.

Good records and documentation also go hand in hand with accurate statistics. Depending on the nature of the grant, organizations may have to document employee salaries, fringe benefits, travel expenses, membership dues, and costs related to equipment and supplies. Copies of receipts, paychecks, and other proof of payments will have to be submitted to be reimbursed by grant funds.

There are various ways to track statistics, and most organizations have a reporting mechanism in place. At the Miller Business Resource Center, we've used a variety of methods depending on the nature of grant. Sometimes we have instituted something as simple as a daily log sheet to capture the number of reference transactions, program registrations, type of patrons assisted, or duration of reference assistance and category of assistance, for example, business versus career, and so on. For other grants, we have had to develop detailed spreadsheets to capture and analyze very specific information, as well as using Google Analytics and Web Access Management to verify the usage of the Miller Business Resource Center's website and database usage.

Philanthropists and Fund-Raising Events

Public libraries in the United States have a history of philanthropic donations dating back to Andrew Carnegie and to present-day philanthropists such as Bill Gates. Of course, not all philanthropists have to be as famous or wealthy to donate their private funds to the library. Libraries need to be proactive in communicating their interests or goals to potential donors and highlighting their past accomplishments. Creating awareness that libraries are good candidates for private funding and capable of following through on specialized projects is also essential. Philanthropic donations can be an unreliable form of funding during hard economic times and can be viewed as unpredictable, since they may not follow the structured guidelines of governmental agencies and corporate foundations. They are useful in initiating new services or programs that the library may have to sustain in the future with the general operating budget or other grant funds.

Fund-raising is typically associated with hospitals, museums, schools, or nonprofits dedicated to a certain cause. In the public library, fund-raising events can be aligned with the mission or goals of a particular institution. In the earlier chapters, we mentioned that under the auspices of the Middle Country Library Foundation, the Miller Business Resource Center hosts two major fund-raising events—Women's Expo and the Strictly Business Tradeshow. Initially, they were developed to reach a particular niche audience that we felt was underserved or would benefit from the services of the business center. Various sponsorship levels and naming opportunities were developed in order to fund both projects, including paying for marketing materials, advertisements, and basic supplies needed to operate the day of the event. Both projects were developed in partnership with other organizations in order to manage the workload and to ensure their success.

8

The Future

On March 1, the ticker running across the CNN broadcast proclaimed, "In bad economic times, libraries flourish." While library attendance figures are rising and we hear more requests for help from patrons, it is also true that tax revenues are down and many libraries are facing budget cuts. How can we best serve those walking through our doors? As unemployment remains high and businesses continue to seek new ways to remain profitable, libraries can assist by developing small business and career information services.

If your library is contemplating starting a business collection and service, you may be viewing it as both a very daunting and a very expensive venture. Most librarians have little business experience and are often intimidated by business questions. However, there are many tutorials, websites, and workshops that can help you become familiar with the basic business resources. The Business Reference Sources and Services Committee (BRASS) of the American Library Association gives a four-week online Business Librarianship 101 course that is inexpensive and covers a variety of business topics including introductory company research, small business and industry research, international business and consumer research, business statistics, and investing and the stock market. The BRASS website also features a committee project, Core Competencies for Business Librarians, which presents annotated bibliographies to subject-specific resources as well as business term definitions and FAQs. An additional project surveys the Best of the Best Business Websites.

Remember, building the business service is a gradual process. If you have the commitment and support of your library administration, as well as your own determination to see it through, you have made a good start. Don't get discouraged!

When interviewing other librarians from public library business centers, we always heard the same mantra. "Reach out to the business organizations in your neighborhood—attend their meetings and describe the service you can offer the business community." Forming alliances with local business service groups such as Chambers of Commerce, Rotary Clubs, and Senior Corps of Retired Executives and partnering with local, state, and federal agencies such as town economic development agencies, county business advisory boards, and small business development corporations not only provides excellent networking opportunities but also allows you to share costs for workshops, seminars, and even trade fairs.

Your goal should be to become so immersed in your area business community that the question is not "Why is the library here?" but "Why isn't the library here?"

BIBLIOGRAPHY

Books

ALA Guide to Economics & Business Reference. Chicago: American Library
    Association, 2011.

Barber, Peggy. *Building a Buzz: Libraries & Word-of-Mouth Marketing.* Chicago:
    American Library Association, 2005.

Berinstein, Paula, and Charles Cotton. *Business Statistics on the Web: Find Them
    Fast at Little or No Cost.* New Jersey: Information Today, 2003.

———. *Finding Statistics Online: The Elusive Numbers You Need.* New Jersey:
    Information Today, 1998.

Bleiweis, Maxine. *Helping Business: The Library's Role in Community Economic
    Development.* New York: Neal-Schuman, 1997.

Boettcher, Jennifer C., and Leonard M. Gaines. *Industry Research Using
    the Economic Census: How to Find It, How to Use It.* Connecticut:
    Greenwood, 2004.

Crawther, Janet L., and Barry Trott. *Partnering with Purpose: A Guide to
    Strategic Partnership Development for Libraries and Other Organizations.*
    Connecticut: Libraries Unlimited, 2004.

Directory of Business Information Resources. 17th ed. New York: Grey House, 2010.

Dobson, Chris, ed. *An Introduction to Online Company Research.* Ohio: Thomson/
    Texere, 2004.

Doity, Kim G. *Rethinking Information Work.* Connecticut: Libraries Unlimited,
    2006.

Doucett, Elizabeth. *Creating Your Library Brand: Communicating Your Relevance
    and Value to Your Patrons.* Chicago: American Library Association, 2009.

Dowd, Nancy, Mary Evangeliste, and Jonathan Silberman. *Bite-Sized Marketing:
    Realistic Solutions for the Overworked Librarian.* Chicago: American
    Library Association, 2009.

Encyclopedia of Business Information Sources. 28th ed. Michigan: Gale, Cengage Learning, 2011.

Fisher, Patricia H., and Marseille M. Pride. *Blueprint for Your Library Marketing Plan: A Guide to Help You Survive and Thrive.* Chicago: American Library Association, 2009.

Jerrard, Jane. *Crisis in Employment: A Librarian's Guide to Helping Job Seekers.* Chicago: American Library Association, 2009.

Kaliski, Burton S., ed. *Encyclopedia of Business and Finance.* 2nd ed. Detroit, MI: Thomson Gale, 2007.

Karp, Rashelle S., ed. *The Basic Business Library: Core Resources.* Connecticut: Greenwood, 2002.

Landau, Herbert B. *Winning Library Grants: A Game Plan.* Chicago: American Library Association, 2010.

Lynch, Sherry. *The Librarian's Guide to Partnerships.* Wisconsin: Highsmith, 1999.

MacKellar, Pamela H., and Stephanie K. Gerding. *Winning Grants: A How-to-Do-It Manual for Librarians with Multimedia Tutorials and Grant Development Tools.* New York: Neal Schuman, 2010.

Macoustra, Jane. *Global Research without Leaving Your Desk: Travelling the World with Your Mouse as Companion.* New York: Neal Schuman, 2010.

Martin, Patricia. *Made Possible By: Succeeding with Sponsorship.* California: Jossey-Bass, 2004.

Miller, Richard K., Kelli Washington, Richard K. Miller and Associates. *Consumer Behavior 2011.* Loganville, GA: Richard K. Miller & Associates. 2011.

——. *Consumer Marketing 2010.* Loganville, GA: Richard K. Miller & Associates, 2010.

——. *The 2011 Entertainment, Media & Advertising Market Research Handbook.* Loganville, GA: Richard K. Miller & Associates, 2011.

——. *The 2011 Healthcare Business Market Research Handbook.* Loganville, GA: Richard K. Miller & Associates, 2011.

——. *The 2010 Leisure Market Research Handbook.* Loganville, GA: Richard K. Miller & Associates, 2010.

——. *The 2011 Restaurant, Food & Beverage Market Research Handbook.* Loganville, GA: Richard K. Miller & Associates, 2011.

——. *The 2010 Retail Business Market Research Handbook.* Loganville, GA: Richard K. Miller & Associates, 2010.

——. *The 2011 Travel & Tourism Market Research Handbook.* Loganville, GA: Richard K. Miller & Associates, 2011.

Moss, Rita W. *Strauss's Handbook of Business Information; A Guide to Librarians, Students and Researchers.* 2nd ed. Connecticut: Libraries Unlimited, 2004.

Murphy, Sarah Anne. *The Librarian as Information Consultant: Transforming Reference for the Information Age.* Chicago: American Library Association, 2011.

Phelps, Marcy, and Mary Ellen Bates. *Research on Main Street: Using the Web to Find Local Business and Market Information.* New Jersey: Information Today, 2011.

Research Alert Yearbook 2011. New York: EPM Communications, 2011.

Riechel, Rosemary. *Public Library Services to Business.* New York: Neal Schuman, 1994.

Ross, Celia. *Making Sense of Business Reference.* Chicago: American Library Association, 2011.

Small Business Sourcebook, 28th ed.: The Entrepreneur's Resource. Detroit, MI: Gale/Cengage Learning. 2011.

Staines, Gail M. *Go Get That Grant! A Practical Guide for Libraries and Nonprofit Organizations.* Maryland: Scarecrow, 2010.

Tucker, Virginia, and Marc Lampson. *Finding the Answers to Legal Questions: A How-to-Do-It Manual.* New York: Neal Schuman, 2010.

Warwick, Mal. *How to Write Successful Funding Letters.* New York: Jossey-Bass, 2001.

Weddle, Peter. *Weddle's Guide to Association Web Sites for Recruiters and HR Professionals, Job Seekers and Career Activists.* Connecticut: Weddle, 2011.

———. *Weddle's 2011/12 Guide to Employment Sites on the Internet.* Connecticut: Weddle, 2011.

White, Gary W., ed. *The Core Business Web: A Guide to Key Information Resources.* New York: Haworth Information, 2004.

Wolfe, Lisa A. *Library Public Relations, Promotions, and Communications: A How-to-Do-It Manual.* 2nd ed. New York: Neal-Schuman, 2005.

Periodicals

Business Information Alert. Alert Publications. Chicago: Alert Publications, 1989–.

Choice: Current Reviews for Academic Libraries. American Library Association. Chicago: American Library Association, 1964–.

Cyberskeptics Guide to Internet Research. Information Today. Medford, NJ: Information Today, 1996–.

The Information Advisor: Analysis, Advice, and Strategy for Business Information Professionals. Information Today. Medford, NJ: Information Today. 1988–.

Information Today. Information Today. Medford, NJ: Information Today. 1984–.

Journal of Business and Finance Librarianship. Binghamton, NY: Haworth, 1990–.

Online. Information Today. Medford, NJ: Information Today. 1987–.

Public Library Quarterly. Binghamton, NY: Haworth, 1979–.

Reference and User Services Quarterly: The Journal of the Reference and User Services Association (RUSA). Chicago: American Library Association. 1960–.

Searcher. Information Today. Medford, NJ: Information Today. 1987.

Articles

Anderson, Mark. "Taking Business (Librarianship) Public." *Journal of Business and Finance Librarianship* 13, no. 3 (2008): 311–19.

Ard, Constance. "Legal Research in the Age of Open Law." *Online* 34, no. 5 (September/October 2010): 29–32.

DiMattia, Susan S. "Getting the Money You Need." *Online* 32, no. 1 (January/February 2008): 22–26.

Erbes, Bill. "Reaching Out with Business-Related Information." *Illinois Libraries* 82, no. 1 (Winter 2000): 40–42.

Hamilton-Pennell, Christine. "Public Libraries and Community Economic Development: Partnering for Success." *Rural Research Report* 18, no. 10 (Winter 2008). www.iira.org/pubs/publications/IIRA_RRR_688.pdf.

Kangiser, Angela. "The Construction Industry Online." *Searcher* 18, no. 5 (June 2010): 12–47.

———. "The Construction Industry Online." *Searcher* 19, no. 2 (March 2011): 40–45.

Keiser, Barbie E. "Free People Searching." *Online* 34, no. 6 (November/December 2010): 19–23.

———. "Hidden Treasures FROM HOOVER'S." *Online* 34, no. 3 (May/June 2010): 40–43.

Leavitt, Laura L., Christine Hamilton-Pennekk, and Barbara Fails. "An Economic Gardening Pilot Project in Michigan: Libraries and Economic Development Agencies Collaborating to Promote Entrepreneurship." *Journal of Business and Finance Librarianship* 15, no. 3/4 (July–December 2010): 208–19.

Lewis, David. "Nongovernmental Organizations, Business, and the Management of Ambiguity." *Nonprofit Management & Leadership* 9, no. 2 (Winter 1988): 135–51.

Lynch, Beverly. "Public Library Service to Business." *Public Libraries* 37, no. 6 (November/December 1998): 382–86.

Miller, Laura. "Why Libraries Still Matter." www.salon.com/books/laura_miller/2011/05/11/nypl_centennial.

Nelson, Patricia. "Libraries Are Players in Economic Development." *PNLA Quarterly* 68, no. 1 (Fall 2003): 19–20.

Ojala, Marydee. "Checklists for Private Company Research." *Online* 35, no. 1 (January/February 2011): 48–50.

Oliver, Lynne. "Qualifications Required for a Library Career Center." *American Libraries* 33, no. 7 (August 2002): 60–61.

Pankl, Robert. "Marketing the Public Library's Business Resources to Small Businesses." *Journal of Business and Finance Librarianship* 15, no. 2 (April–June 2010): 94–103.

Ross, Celia. "Online Resources for Business Research." *Choice* 44, no. 8 (April 2007): 1271–85.

Runde, Dan. "How to Make Development Partnerships Work." *OECD Observer* 255 (May 2006): 29–31.

Shapiro, Phil. "Public Libraries as Business Incubators." *PC World,* June 2, 2010. www.pcworld.com/businesscenter/article/197759/public_libraries_as_business_incubators.html

University of Kansas Policy Research Institute. "The Role of Public Libraries in Local Economic Development." Report no. 260 (November 2000). www.ipsr.ku.edu/resrep/pdf/m260/pdf.

Welch, Jeanie M. "Silent Partners: Public Libraries and Their Services to Small Businesses and Entrepreneurs." *Public Libraries,* September/October 2005, 282–85.

Wisdom, Gavin. "Libraries Help Bottom Line." *The Durano Herald,* February 18, 2001. www.durangoherald.com/article/20110220/NEWS04/702209977/0/FRONTPAGE/Libraries-help-bottomline.

Womack, Ryan. "The Orientation and Training of New Librarians for Business Information." *Journal of Business and Finance Librarianship* 13, no. 3 (2008): 217–29.

Zarsky, Terry. "Instruction for the Business Community." *Colorado Libraries* 26, no. 4 (Winter 2000): 38–39.

INDEX